CYNTHIA W
HOT AND SPICY COOKING

Cynthia Wine's
HOT & SPICY
COOKING

Cynthia Wine

 PENGUIN BOOKS

PENGUIN BOOKS
Published by the Penguin Group
Penguin Books Canada Ltd, 10 Alcorn Avenue, Toronto,
Ontario, Canada M4V 3B2
Penguin Books Ltd, 27 Wrights Lane, London W8 5TZ, England
Penguin Books USA Inc., 375 Hudson Street, New York, New York 10014, U.S.A.
Penguin Books Australia Ltd, Ringwood, Victoria, Australia
Penguin Books (NZ) Ltd, 182-190 Wairau Road, Auckland 10,
New Zealand

Penguin Books Ltd, Registered Offices: Harmondsworth, Middlesex, England

Published in Penguin Books, 1984

3 5 7 9 10 8 6 4 2

Canadian Cataloguing in Publication Data

Wine, Cynthia.
  Cynthia Wine's hot & spicy cooking

ISBN 0-14-046654-1

1. Cookery, International. I. Title. II. Title: Hot &
spicy cooking.

TX725.A1W56 1984   641.59   C84-098294-1

*Drawings on reverse side of
photo inserts by
Rick Carty
Book design by
Catherine Wilson/Sunkisst Graphics
Photography by
Hal Roth Photography
Food stylist
Judy Wells
Manufactured in Canada by
Gagne Printing Limited
Typesetting by
Jay Tee Graphics Ltd.*

Contents

For Ford: whose love of spice made this book possible and whose refusal to eat out every night made it necessary.

ACKNOWLEDGEMENTS

This project began as hundreds of bits of paper and bags of funny spices. It became a reliable and thorough book thanks to the collaboration of:

Kathy Chute who tested recipes, and her family who tasted them. With the authority of her cooking expertise and Venezuelan background, she provided much information.

Mary Adachi who edited, unmuddled the muddled (and the metric), and gave hours of suggestion and support.

Heather Nirenberg who typed and retyped, without ever once asking why we couldn't get it right the first time.

Some helped smooth the path, among them Dawn Berney, Sheila Kieran, Desmond Poon, Elisebeth Escobar, and Robert Kearns. The contributions of others are named with the recipes they kindly gave.

A NOTE ON METRICATION

The recipes in this book are given in both imperial and metric measures. The metric measurements are not exact conversions of the imperial measurements but have been rounded off to standard metric units. The basic proportion of ingredients remains consistent.

Introduction

The first time I ever heard the expression "mouth hunger" was in relation to hot and spicy food. A man at the next table in a Chinese restaurant was coaxing his wife into ordering the orange chicken with chilies instead of the chow mein. "I want something spicy," he explained. "Chow mein will fill me up, but it won't fix my mouth hunger." She knew just what he meant, and so did I. To describe such yearning of the mouth in that way is to conjure up a picture of dozens of tiny taste buds banging their little knives and forks on the palate, demanding a jolt that can be satisfied only by a blast of flavour.

In recent years it has been easy enough to quiet the unruly buds in the increasing numbers of restaurants offering Szechuan, Indian, Mexican and Cajun food. This book is to show you that you can calm the craving at your own kitchen table. It is also designed to show you that there is a world of spice outside of Indian, Mexican and Chinese food. Many of the foods you've eaten bland, can be prodded into new potency with the addition of spice.

For those of us raised in northern climes, the leap to preparing hot foods, rather than ordering them, may not be an easy one to make. Five years ago I no more would have chopped a chili than I would have jumped from a jet. It's because most of us grew up suspicious of spice. At our house, where sage was daring, an aging bottle of Tabasco sat senile behind cupboard doors and pepper was a grey dust that came in small jars.

I'll bet at your house, like mine, chili peppers were as distant as Chile. They simply weren't what you learned to love at your mother's knee, unless, of course, your mother's knee was in Mexico or some place where people ate hot foods and started revolutions.

The increasing popularity of hot spicy foods, even in countries where the snow falls, fits the philosophical climate of the times. This is an age of pleasure pushed to the point of pain. We run marathons until our muscles howl, then thrill in the high that follows; we admire the notion of a hot sauna followed by a roll in the snow. Hot and spicy food is like that. To eat a Szechuan soup or an Indian vindaloo for the first time is to risk a reaction one never expected from food. Food is supposed to comfort, not startle, to soothe, rather than stimulate.

When it is properly prepared, hot food will be pleasantly stimulating, but not punishing. It is not there to test your mettle or your tolerance for suffering. Food should not be made so hot that all you taste is spice and all you feel is pain. Hot spices should complement the dish, give it a lift and a variation of flavour.

The line between pain and pleasure derived from hot food is personal. You will notice that your tolerance level rises and hunger for spice increases the more you eat it. Some people go to extremes to fulfill their craving. In Dublin, Ireland, an East Indian restaurant called The Taj Mahal lists on its menu ''Vindaloo Michael O'Doibhlin'', a dish developed solely for a customer whose amazing lust for spice could not be satisfied by that restaurant's regular offerings. They spiced their vindaloo, normally an extraordinarily spicy dish, beyond the bounds of ordinary human tolerance and named it just for him.

There are those who swear that very spicy food is good for the soul — that it lifts the spirits as it provokes the palate. There are even those who suggest it's an aphrodisiac. Well, maybe. What's more provable is that it does seem to be a healthy sort of food. Dishes that are highly seasoned with intense spices tend to be relatively low in salt and fat. There is very little salt in the recipes in this book, and much of that is optional.

The spices themselves are high in vitamins. Paprika, for one, is thought to have proportionally more Vitamin C than fresh lemon. Chili peppers are loaded with the stuff. (Anything *that* good for you is bound to hurt.)

The search for adventure in food and for menus high in flavour and low in fat and salt has furthered the fortunes of spicy food, even in countries like Canada and Ireland, where the native cuisines could hardly be called spicy. Most of the hot cuisines were developed in southern, hot countries. Even within a country, dishes tend to get hotter the further south their origins. For example, the food of southern India is hotter than that of the north, though northern cuisine is no mean slouch. There are several theories to explain why people from hot countries prefer hot food, but most lovers of spice would simply answer that they love it because it hurts so good:

- In countries like India, with its intense heat and limited refrigeration facilities, it was discovered that highly spiced food spoiled less rapidly.

- Eating hot spices makes you perspire, thus triggering the body's natural cooling mechanism.

- Chilies are rich in Vitamin C, so it may be a case of satisfying the body's need for vitamins from sources most readily available.

It will be apparent to anyone who samples a variety of spicy cuisines, that though they may have different features, they have many common attributes. Hot foods are usually served in smaller quantities than mild and are accompanied by foods designed to either complement or neutralize the hot spices. Rice is commonly used in Asian countries to soak up hot sauces and provide background for them. Naan, a flat bread used in India, or tortillas of Mexico provide the same starchy service. Tomatoes feature heavily in many hot cuisines because they behave so well with spicy food; their slightly acidic taste provides a good foil.

In some cuisines a dish in itself may not be particularly hot, but condiments served as accompaniment provide the piquancy. The Indonesians use sambal, a concoction based mostly on chilies. East Indians provide a series of relishes so intensely hot that after one taste, I think my ears are bleeding.

All cuisines which are very hot use chili peppers (capsicum) in varying degrees in fresh, liquid or powdered form. The distinctive flavours of each cuisine come from the other spices which are used in concert with the chilies. For example, a basic Chinese flavouring would include ginger root and soy sauce; Mexican cookery uses limes; an Indonesian dish would include peanuts, soy sauce and ginger root.

Knowing that these varied hot cuisines have common denominators should make things somewhat easier for the neophyte gingerly approaching this new world of cooking. You may take further comfort from the philosophy of folk singer Arlo Guthrie's friend Alice May Brock who said: ''Don't be intimidated by foreign cookery. Tomatoes and oregano make it Italian; wine and tarragon make it French. Sour cream makes it Russian, lemon and cinnamon make it Greek. Soy sauce makes it Chinese; garlic makes it good. Now you are an International Cook.''

It's the same for hot foods. Don't be afraid of them. Peppers make it painful; rice makes it nice. As long as you know the agents of heat and their coolants, you will be forearmed. The recipes in this book are prepared medium to hot. Even if you're like Michael O'Doibhlin and you're sure you like your food exceedingly spicy, please taste the dish before you add more chilies — it may be hot enough as it is. If you want to begin cautiously, reduce the amount of hot spice before you start. In testing and tasting the recipes, we found that our own tolerance increased as we went along.

Agents of Heat

These are the agents that demand attention. If you don't give them attention before you eat them, you'll require attention after you have put them in your mouth. However, properly used, they are the agents of intense pleasure and will give you the sense of really being alive.

CHILI PEPPERS

Chili peppers have earned a section all their own because they are the primary source of heat and pain in food. They are also a primary source of pain outside the alimentary canal, as anyone who has touched the inside of a chili, then rubbed an eye, can tell you. It is important that they be chosen and handled with deference to their power.

Chilies have a big army. They are part of the capsicum family which encompasses several species and hundreds of varieties. They may range from tame (bell peppers) to torrid (cayenne peppers). You may be surprised at how many can be found fresh in urban marketplaces, even in northern climates. They go by many names and come in various shapes. In this book, we have restricted the use of chilies to those that are easily found canned or dried, if not fresh.

The fresh chilies you are most likely to encounter in the produce section of North American stores outside of California and Texas will be yellow, green or red in colour and long and narrow. Ethnic markets, especially those specializing in east or west Indian or Mexican foods, will offer a much wider range. A good rule of thumb is that the smaller, darker and narrower the pepper, the hotter it will be. Generally, green chili, the unripe fruit, is crisper and hotter than the ripe red chili (as red bell peppers are sweeter than green).

But this is only a very general rule meant to make the array a little less daunting. There are some dangerous exceptions — ancho peppers, which can be as large as bell peppers, pack a wallop. Others sneak up on you. During testing for this book, I bit into a largish, long green pepper that looked just like a mild banana pepper I had chewed the day before. I will remember that feckless nibble for the rest of my days. Always test the chili cautiously — touch the tip of the chili with your finger, then touch the tip of your tongue, or lightly lick the end of the pepper. Whether mild or hot, fresh chilies taste better and are more fun than the preserved, so don't be afraid to experiment. Don't bother looking for just one kind of pepper; take what comes and treat it with caution. Most of the hot peppers are interchangeable.

Among dried red chilies, you may find anchos, cayenne, pequín or even the Japanese hontaka peppers if you're lucky, but it's most likely you will encounter a variety of the dried new hybrids grown in California. Store dried peppers in airtight containers away from light.

Properly stored, they should keep their flavours indefinitely. Red pepper flakes, the dried and flaked pods and flesh of the capsicum (chili pepper) are available in even the most perfunctory spice sections of grocery stores. Red pepper flakes are quite hot, especially the seeds, so they can be used wherever chili peppers are required.

Canned or bottled peppers may be more easily found than dried or fresh. It's worth buying a jar or can of the jalapeño peppers, if only for the amazing jelly it makes. If they are in brine, rinse the chilies in cold water before using. Jalapeños also make an excellent addition to a dish of chili. Usually the seeds, veins and stems are removed and the flesh chopped up finely. The other canned or dried green pepper you might encounter is the serrano. Approach it with caution; it will bring you to your knees. Canned chilies, once opened, should be transferred to an airtight jar and kept in the refrigerator.

PREPARING CHILI PEPPERS

1 First, put on a pair of rubber gloves or surgical gloves and don't pretend you know better. Never rub your eyes or any other part of your face with gloves that have touched chilies. The volatile oils can cause a burn blister that looks and feels like the real thing. If you do get a burn, rinse the area thoroughly with warm water and wash with soap, then rinse with cool water. If it still stings, apply burn ointment. If you get a slight sting, pressing the inside of a banana skin on the affected area will help.

2 With either fresh, dried or canned chilies, it is often advisable to discard the pods, seeds and stem. These are the hottest parts, so hot that they can paralyze the palate and detract from the flavour of the flesh. If the skin is tough and it's the inside flesh you're after, you get to it by broiling the chili until it blisters, then peeling it.

3 Fresh chilies gain extra flavour if they are roasted over a gas or barbecue flame and allowed to steam in a towel. If you are roasting the pepper over an open flame, be careful not to inhale the fumes from the pepper.

4 Large dried chilies should be torn into bits and soaked in hot water for 30 minutes. They can be puréed in a processor with some of the water, if you wish.

CAYENNE

The name is derived from its origins in Cayenne, the chief town of French Guiana. The cayenne pepper is red, long and very hot. To make the product we buy in jars, the seeds and pod of the pepper are ground to a very fine powder. A few dashes of the pepper should do the trick, since it is very hot to most palates. Overuse may create a bitter taste.

GARLIC

Its effect on the palate depends on how roughly it's treated. Generally, the harder you hit it, the harder it hits back. Roasted whole in its skin, garlic is as sweet and docile as a mother's love. Slightly bruised, it's slightly tart. Skinned and chopped, it's pungent. Smashed with the flat of a knife, it begins to bite. Smeared by the blade of a food processor, it releases its sting and the taster really feels it. Most recipients of garlic breath find that the bulb does violence no matter how gently it's prepared. Addicted consumers will find an antidote in the aphorism: ''The man who eats parsley need not eat garlic sparsely.''

GINGER

This tan-coloured, gnarled root has a strong and peppery bite, particularly when it's fresh. Most of the ginger we buy is a native of the warmer parts of Asia, though some consider the Jamaican ginger to be superior. Green ginger, the root we buy for Chinese cookery, comes from the lower portion of the stem and root stock. It must be peeled before it is added to soups or other dishes. The portions nearest the stem, known as stem ginger, are more delicate in flavour and are usually preserved in heavy syrup or crystallized in sugar. The lower portions that aren't used for green ginger are sun dried and sold in pieces or powdered (this is the ground ginger we buy in jars). Ground ginger is useful for flavouring baked desserts, but should be rejected in favour of the fresh for cookery. Unpeeled ginger can be stored sealed in a plastic bag or foil in the refrigerator. Ginger can be peeled, wrapped in foil and stored in the freezer, then grated, unthawed, whenever required.

HORSERADISH

An herb of the mustard family, horseradish is often used in concert with mustard to add fire to both. On its own, if it's fresh, horseradish needs little help. When it's fresh, it has a bite that can make your eyeballs ache. In some countries like Russia, Finland, and Poland, it is simply grated and served with meats, but more often it is mixed with fresh or sour cream. The Gay Hussar, a Hungarian restaurant in London, England, serves freshly grated horseradish in cream along with spicy sausage for a memorable appetizer. In ancient times, horseradish was despised because it was thought to be bitter, stringy, difficult to digest, and dissolved the enamel on the teeth. Now we know it just feels that way. Wrapped in foil, fresh horseradish freezes well. Grate it while it's frozen hard.

MUSTARD

The seeds of the mustard plant, left whole, are quite tame, but when crushed, they become the pungent spice which gives Welsh rarebit its kick. Prepared mustards are made from ground mustard seeds blended with vinegar or other liquid and herbs and other seasonings. They come in a host of flavours, textures and colours. You can make one of the hottest pastes available merely by mixing the powdered mustard with a bit of boiling water, and letting it rest for 10 minutes. Even so, mustard needs help from chilies if a dish is to be really hot. Too much mustard may give a bitter taste. Despite its bite, prepared mustard as we know it today began in a country not commonly known for its pungent food. Mrs. Clements of Durham, England, was the first to grind up the seeds in a mill just like wheat flour. It formed the basis of the Durham mustard we know today. She kept her recipe secret for years and made her reputation travelling from town to town on horseback. George I was one of her first patrons.

PAPRIKA

It is made from a variety of capsicum and is a cousin to cayenne and other chili peppers. The powder is made from the whole pod, stems and seeds of the dried pepper. Paprika originated in South America, and around 1585 it was taken to Hungary where it was accepted with alacrity; it is as popular now as then. Hungarian paprika is still considered to be the best. It comes in varying strengths and quality, of which rose is the best quality. The Spanish paprika, commonly used in North America, is very mild and used more for garnish than for flavouring. If you want to make a paprika dish hotter than the recipe suggests, don't add more paprika or the dish may become bitter. Add some Tabasco or red pepper flakes instead.

The paprika pepper is rich in Vitamins A and C. In 1937 Professor Szent-Gyotgi was awarded the Nobel Prize for finding a new vitamin in paprika which he called Vitamin P. He also proved that the pepper contained more Vitamin C than citrus fruits.

PEPPER

Next to salt, pepper is the most universal condiment and one of the first to be introduced to Europe from the east. Pepper is a berry which grows mainly in India. Though it shares a common name with chilies, it otherwise bears no relation. (It is thought that Columbus named chilies as ''peppers'' to convince Queen Isabella that he had found a new version of the pepper that she prized.)

Black pepper is gathered from the dried, unripe fruit of the piper nigrum. White pepper is the same berry with its outer husk removed. White pepper is quite mild, its use reserved mainly for esthetes who can't bear the sight of black pepper flakes in white sauce. Good peppercorns should be hard, even in colour, and free from stems or stalks. Whole peppercorns should be stored in airtight jars and will keep indefinitely. Commercially ground black pepper loses potency quickly and isn't a patch on the freshly ground. Peppercorns can be crushed in a mortar and pestle or, if you want a lot of them, in a food processor or coffee grinder. The coffee grinder is best if you need several teaspoons of finely ground black pepper. (Be sure to clean out the coffee grounds first — and the pepper after — to avoid taste surprises.)

The pink and green peppercorns currently enjoying fashion are the berries from the piper nigrum at various stages of maturity. They have no real heat and will do more for your status than they can for your recipe.

Szechuan peppercorns are the reddish-brown fragrant peppercorns native to Szechuan province in China. They are sold dried and can be found in specialty stores. Before use, toast them in a small skillet until their fragrance is released. Their effect is more numbing than burning. They are not as hot as the black peppercorn from the piper nigrum. The hotness in Szechuan food is not primarily from Szechuan peppercorns, but from chili peppers.

COMMERCIAL MIXTURES

CURRY POWDER
The word ''curry'' derives from the Indian word ''kari'' and simply means ''sauce''. The way the word has come to be used, it means nothing of the sort: Generally it refers to a combination of spices used in Indian food. This combination traditionally is homemade and hand-ground and varies as to district and dish.

Most commercial curry powders have a distinctive taste of their own, and while that taste is often fine, it bears little resemblance to the combination of spices used for the real thing. (See the chapter on condiments and relishes for a recipe for the real thing.) Though the formula used by each manufacturer varies, the basic components in a commercial curry powder are cumin, coriander, cayenne, turmeric (which gives it its yellow colour) and black pepper. Many of the commercial powders are quite mild, but those that are stronger usually contain ginger and ground chili peppers. Purists sometimes decry the use of commercial preparations, though some use a little of both and achieve a happy compromise.

CHILI POWDER

Chili powder is included in this list of hot commercial preparations only because it sounds as though it should be hot. The packaged chili powder found most often in our supermarkets isn't hot at all. It is usually prepared from sweet peppers, cumin, cayenne (only a bit for colour) and often includes some salt as a carrier. You might run across some chili powders prepared from chili peppers, with corn flour as an extender. In any case, none is a patch on one you might make yourself from a similar combination of spices ground in a processor, coffee grinder, or crushed in a mortar and pestle.

CHILI SAUCES

Like chili powder, the bottled sauce which looks like catsup with seeds is made from sweet peppers and sugar and has no real heat at all. But if you look closely among the condiments in the gourmet sections of supermarkets or in specialty stores, you will find chili sauces made from torrid chilies, like Szechuan chili sauce. You will be happier with these.

TABASCO

Did you hear the one about the couple who were together so long they were on their second bottle of Tabasco? This traditional liquid pepper sauce contains only Tabasco peppers (developed just for this purpose), vinegar and salt. It has a shelf life of five to six years (as long as many couples have). The condiment has been produced by the McIlhenny family in Louisiana since 1868. It was formulated originally to flavour creole and gumbos, but now is used world-wide to hot up lots of dishes. There are other liquid pepper preparations on the market. Read the ingredients to make sure they have what you want.

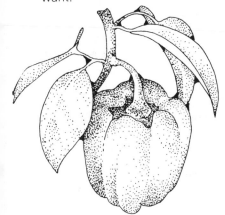

Accompaniments and Poultices: How to eat food that bites back

When the mouth starts to burn, the first inclination is to gulp water in an attempt to dilute or even drown the spice. It doesn't work. Water may take away the heat for a minute, but it does nothing for the sting except spread it. If you have bitten off more than you can chew, the fastest poultice is a spoonful of rice or a bite of bread. In extreme cases, a lick of some plain, granulated sugar will complete the job.

But the best policy is planning and prevention.

- When ordering in a restaurant or planning a meal at home, the best rule of tongue is that courses proceed from mildly spiced to heavily spiced. The idea is that the palate should be gradually acclimatized to the spice. An Indian dinner might begin with dal, a bland purée of lentils and proceed to Tandoori chicken and then to hot meat and vegetable curries. If you began with the hot curries, your palate might be paralyzed to the nuances of the milder dishes. If your meal is to include a spicy soup followed by a spicy main course, be gentle with the soup spices, or it won't matter if you're serving cardboard for the second course.

- The dishes you serve with the spicy food should provide contrast in temperature and taste: Coarsely grated cheese or a dollop of sour cream takes the bite out of an aggressive bowl of chili; a tomato and onion salad is crunchy and reassuring with a hot curried meat; a dollop of plain yoghurt is bland and cooling against a cheeky curry or a highly spiced soup. These are more than just affable accompaniments. The contrast itself gives delight akin to a chilled martini sipped in a hot tub.

This yoghurt-mint raita is a good example. It is cold and crunchy and more herbal than spicy — in other words, everything that the curries it accompanies are not:

YOGHURT-MINT RAITA

Yoghurt	2 cups (500 mL)
Onion	1 medium, grated
Fresh mint	1 Tbsp (15 mL) finely chopped
Salt	1/2 tsp (2 mL)
Freshly ground pepper	to taste
Cucumbers	2, peeled and sliced paper-thin

1 In a bowl, blend together yoghurt, onion, mint, salt, and freshly ground pepper. Gently fold in cucumber slices. Chill thoroughly before serving.

Serves 4

• Dessert after a spicy meal should be light, cooling and kind, probably fruity. In fact, fresh, chilled fruit — grapes, an orange, a pineapple or a mango are about as good an ending as you might want. I have found fruit custards surprisingly good, though purists might eschew them. I find the mango custard which Jennifer Bannerjee always serves after a fiery East Indian meal so good that I'm inclined to skip the meal and go right to it.

MANGO CUSTARD

Whole milk	2 cups (500 mL)
Whipping cream	1 cup (250 mL)
Sugar	3 Tbsp (50 mL)
Fresh or canned mango purée	1 1/2 cups (375 mL)

1 Combine milk, whipping cream, and sugar in a saucepan. Bring to a boil. Reduce heat and simmer for 1 hour, or until reduced to 1 1/4 cups (300 mL). Strain.

2 Blend in mango purée and chill.

Serves 4

Sherbert is terrific to keep on hand, both as a dessert or as a quick poultice for someone who has waded in beyond his or her depth.

PINEAPPLE SHERBERT

Very ripe fresh pineapple	1 large
Water	1 cup (250 mL)
Sugar	1/2 cup (125 mL)

1 Peel and core pineapple. Cut into small pieces and purée in a blender or food processor. This should yield approximately 3 cups (750 mL) purée.

2 Combine with water and sugar. Process until well mixed.

3 Pour the mixture into ice trays and freeze until partially frozen.

4 Turn mixture into a bowl and beat until smooth. Return to trays and freeze until firm but not hard. Garnish with fresh mint leaves.

Serves 4-6

What to drink with what you eat

Because spicy food tends to make you thirsty, what you drink is more than just a question of flavour esthetics. Champagne, fruity white wines, and green tea in tiny cups are lovely with hot Chinese food or any food for that matter, and they'll add class to the table, but you hardly want to guzzle them. Beer is better for that, especially light beer. The lower alcohol content allows you to gulp, but still keep your capacity to taste and your wits about you as the meal progresses. So does this light sangría from Chile's Mexican Flavors in Toronto. Fruit chunks, common to many sangrías, are excluded from this recipe so as not to slow down the fast drinker.

SANGRÍA

Water	2 cups (500 mL)
Brown sugar	3/4 cup (175 mL)
Cloves	6, whole
Orange zest	from 2 oranges
Lemon zest	from 2 limes
Dry red wine	1 bottle (750 mL)
Dry white wine	1 bottle (750 mL)
Soda water	1 bottle (750 mL)

1 In a saucepan combine the water, brown sugar, cloves, and fruit zests. Boil together until the mixture reduces to half, about 5-7 minutes. Strain and cool.

2 In a large pitcher or bowl, combine the syrup mixture with the red and white wines and stir thoroughly. Refrigerate until cold.

3 Just before serving add the soda water.

Serves 4-6

If you're gulping for poultice, a plain fruit juice is probably most effective. A slightly acidic juice like orange is best, but dilute it with soda so the juice doesn't fill you up too quickly. Fruit juices seem to go best with dishes that contain a lot of chilies, though I like fruit drinks less with curries. This melon seed drink goes with both and is the most effective liquid extinguisher I know, especially if you use cantaloupe.

MELON SEED DRINK

Fresh melon seeds (cantaloupe are best)	1 cup (250 mL)
Water	6 cups (1.5 L)
Lime rind	grated rind of 1 lime
Sugar	1 cup (250 mL)

1 Place seeds in an electric blender and process until very fine.

2 Combine the seeds with the water, grated rind, and sugar in a large covered jug. Let sit for 4 hours.

3 Strain through a piece of damp muslim or several thicknesses of damp cheesecloth. Squeeze to extract all the milk from the seeds.

4 Serve over ice.

Serves 4-6

With curries, a yoghurt drink works best. This one is lovely.

BORANI

Yoghurt	1 cup (250 mL)
Cold water	2 cups (500 mL)
Lemon peel	4 strips
Fresh mint leaves	1 tsp (5 mL)
Salt	to taste
Freshly ground pepper	to taste

1 Combine ingredients in a cocktail shaker or bowl. Shake or whisk until blended. Serve in chilled glasses.

Serves 4

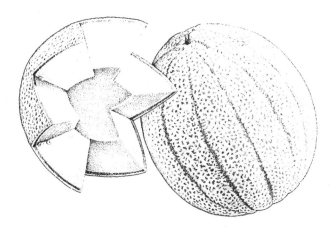

Spicy Drinks

We're probably most familiar with the spicy, tomato juice based drinks which begin with Bloody and end with Mary or Caesar. The vodka in them is particularly receptive to spurts of fiery Tabasco, but if you'll experiment, you'll find that many other hard liquors, like Tequila, Bourbon and even gin, warm to a touch of liquid pepper.

There are times, though, that you may want the warmth without the whammy, the bite without the blast. These two temperate brews were contributed by Elisebeth Escobar at Chile's Mexican Flavors in Toronto. She says the chili tea is a cold cure and the ginger tea will fix anything else. Brew up a cup and read on.

CHILI TEA

Water	1 1/4 cups (300 mL)
Strong chili powder	1/2 tsp (2 mL)
Ground cinnamon	1/4 tsp (1 mL)
Ground nutmeg	1/4 tsp (1 mL)
Ground cloves	1/2 tsp (2 mL)
Fresh lemon juice	1 Tbsp (15 mL)
Honey	to taste

1 Bring water to the boil, add spices and simmer very slowly for 4-5 minutes. Strain through coffee filter paper, if desired. Season to taste with honey. Use for colds or the flu; it must be spicy enough to cause sweating.

GINGER TEA

Water	1 1/4 cups (300 mL)
Fresh ginger root	1/2 tsp (2 mL) peeled and grated
Fresh lemon juice	1 Tbsp (15 mL)
Ground cloves	1/4 tsp (1 mL)
Honey	to taste

1 Bring water to the boil, add the spices and simmer very slowly for 10 minutes. Strain through a coffee filter, if desired. Season to taste with honey. Makes one serving.

APPETIZERS

HOUMOUS

A well-known and much loved Middle Eastern dish of chick peas, sesame paste, and lemon juice. The nutty peas are worked to the consistency of mayonnaise as they are blended with the juice and paste. This recipe has extra jolt from lots of garlic and red chilies. Serve it spread on a platter and decorated with ripe black olives and radish flowers. Edge the platter with freshly cut triangles of pita bread which are folded into cones to spoon up this special appetizer.

Dried chick peas	1 cup (250 mL)
Baking soda	1 tsp (5 mL)
Water	1 1/4 cups (300 mL)
Fresh lemon juice	6-8 Tbsp (90-120 mL)
Salt	1 tsp (5 mL)
Garlic	1 clove
Water	3/4 cup (175 mL)
Tahini (sesame paste)	1/4 cup (50 mL)
Fresh hot red chilies	2, finely chopped
Fresh parsley	1 Tbsp (25 mL) finely chopped
Olive oil	1/4 cup (50 mL) or to taste

1 Place chick peas in a large bowl. Cover with water and add baking soda. Soak overnight. Drain chick peas, rinse, then drain again.

2 Place chick peas in a large saucepan. Add 1 1/4 cups (300 mL) water and bring to a boil. Cover and simmer for 1 hour, or until the peas are very tender. Drain and purée in a blender with lemon juice, salt, garlic, 3/4 cup (175 mL) water and tahini.

3 Spoon houmous onto a platter, spread it flat and sprinkle with finely chopped hot red chilies and parsley. Drizzle olive oil on top. Serve with pita.

Serves 4

TZADZIKI

A piquant and garlicky condiment served as an appetizer with pita bread or as an accompaniment to lamb kebob.

Yoghurt	1 cup (250 mL)
Garlic	10 cloves, peeled and minced
Lemon juice	1 Tbsp (15 mL)

1 Combine all ingredients.

2 Refrigerate for several hours before serving to allow flavours to blend.

Serves 2-4

EGGPLANT CAVIAR

This dip, sometimes called poor man's caviar, is popular in countries like the Balkans where eggplants flourish. There are many versions of it: This is one of the spiciest. Traditionally, the whole eggplant is roasted over an open flame until the skin bursts to give it a smoky flavour. If this method is impractical, it may be baked according to instructions here.

Eggplant	2 small
Fresh lemon juice	4 Tbsp (60 mL)
Olive oil	4 Tbsp (60 mL)
Garlic	1 large clove
Paprika	1/4 tsp (1 mL)
Cayenne	1/2 tsp (2 mL)
Scallion	1, finely minced
Tomato	1, seeded and chopped
Salt	1 tsp (5 mL) or to taste
Freshly ground pepper	1/2 tsp (2 mL) or to taste

1 Pierce eggplant in several places. Bake at 400°F (200°C) for about 30 minutes, or until very soft. Split eggplant open and remove the pulp.

2 In a blender, place the eggplant pulp, lemon juice, olive oil, garlic, paprika, and cayenne. Blend until smooth and light. Stir in scallions and tomato. Season with salt and freshly ground pepper.

3 Serve it as an appetizer with thick chunks of dark bread, crackers or fresh vegetables.

Yields approximately 2 1/2 cups (625 mL), serves 4

CREAM CHEESE WITH JALAPEÑOS (CHILI CON QUESO)

A Mexican dish with spicy, fast-food appeal. The compelling combination of cream cheese, chilies and tomatoes yields a hot dip with the consistency of thick mayonnaise. Serve it as an appetizer with corn chips or as a luncheon dish with refried beans and crisp tortillas.

Butter	2 Tbsp (25 mL)
Onion	1 large, finely minced
Tomatoes	2, peeled, seeded and chopped
Cream cheese	8 oz (250 g)
Heavy cream	3/4 cup (175 mL)
Pickled jalapeño peppers	1 cup (250 mL) chopped
Salt	1/2 tsp (2 mL) or to taste
Bacon	4 slices, crisply cooked and crumbled (optional)

1 Melt butter in a skillet and cook the onion until soft. Add the tomatoes and cook for 15 minutes over medium heat until sauce is thick.

2 Add the cheese, cream and jalapeño peppers and stir over low heat until cheese has melted completely. Do not boil. Season with salt. Pour into a serving dish and sprinkle with crumbled bacon, if desired.

Serves 4

BRANDADE DE MORUE

This spread is based on a classic Provençal dish of salt cod blended with cream and oil until not one flake of fish is discernable. This version is spiked with cayenne and extra garlic. Serve it as an appetizer or main dish. Leftovers can be dipped in breadcrumbs and fried in butter to make fishcakes.

Salt cod	1 1/2 lbs (675 g), soaked overnight in cold water
Hot mashed potatoes	2 cups (500 mL), without added milk or butter
Whipping cream	1 cup (250 mL), at room temperature
Warm olive oil	1/4 cup (50 mL)
Cayenne	1 tsp (5 mL)
Garlic	5 large cloves, finely minced

1 Drain salt cod and place in a saucepan; add enough cold water to cover. Bring to a boil and simmer for 20 minutes. Drain cod and carefully remove the skin and bones. Flake fish.

2 In a bowl, beat the potatoes and cod with an electric mixer. Continue beating while adding the cream and olive oil. Add the cayenne and garlic and finish whipping briefly on high speed.

3 Serve as an appetizer with freshly made toast points or Melba toast. This can also be served as a main dish with sliced tomatoes and lemon wedges.

Serves 10 as an appetizer or 4-5 as a main course

GUACAMOLE

Although this version of Mexican guacamole is more spicy than soothing, it offers all the pleasures of this classic salad of fresh avocados blended with tomatoes and garlic. Serve freshly made with corn chips or toasted tortillas.

Avocados	2 medium
Fresh lime juice	3 Tbsp (50 mL)
Fresh lemon juice	1 Tbsp (15 mL)
Garlic	3 cloves, finely minced
Scallions	2, finely minced
Tomato	1 medium, diced
Pickled jalapeño peppers	4, seeded and minced
Chili powder	1/2 tsp (2 mL)
Fresh coriander	2 sprigs, finely chopped (optional)
Salt	1 tsp (5 mL) or to taste
Freshly ground pepper	1/2 tsp (2 mL) or to taste

1 Peel and pit the avocados. Mash with a fork until smooth. Do not purée in a blender; the texture will not be right. Add the rest of the ingredients and mix well. If not using immediately, cover with plastic wrap so it will not turn brown at the edges.

Yields about 3 cups (750 mL)

SESAME DIP

You'll swear there's peanut butter in it, but there isn't — just sesame seeds, fresh ginger, and honey. This is the best dip you'll ever eat. It's based on a recipe from Mullen & Cie., a Toronto catering firm; they serve it with an overflowing basket of raw vegetables.

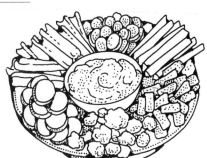

Sesame seeds	2 Tbsp (25 mL)
Soy sauce	1/4 cup (50 mL)
Egg	1 raw
Liquid honey	4 1/2 tsp (22 mL)
Vegetable oil (not olive)	1 1/4 cups (300 mL)
Sesame oil	2 tsp (10 mL)
Fresh ginger root	1/2-inch (1-cm) cube or 1/2 tsp (2 mL) powdered
Szechuan chili sauce or cayenne	1 1/2 tsp (7 mL)

1 Toast sesame seeds in a small skillet until they are golden brown.

2 Combine sesame seeds, soy sauce, egg, and honey in a food processor or blender and process while slowly adding vegetable oil, in droplets, through the processor feed tube or hole in the top of the blender jar.

3 Add sesame oil, ginger, and Szechuan chili sauce or cayenne. Mix well.

Yields approximately 2 cups (500 mL)

RADISHES WITH SOUR CREAM

The crunch of fresh radishes and the cool flavour of sour cream are contrasted with the bite of horseradish. This is good with spiced meats or as a side dish with curried vegetables. It looks pretty garnished with radish roses and watercress.

Red radishes	2 cups (500 mL) thinly sliced
Salt	1/2 tsp (2 mL)
Sour cream	2/3 cup (150 mL)
Prepared horseradish	4 tsp (20 mL) drained
Sugar	1/2 tsp (2 mL)

1 Place sliced radishes in a bowl and cover with cold water. Add salt and let stand at room temperature for 1 hour.

2 Drain and rinse radishes. Dry on paper towels.

3 Mix together sour cream, horseradish and sugar. Toss radish slices with sour cream and serve immediately.

Serves 4

INDIAN SAMOSA

Every nation seems to have its way of gift-wrapping bits of savoury food: The Italians have ravioli, the Chinese, wonton; Eastern Euro-peans have pyrohy and East Indians, samosa. The samosa is a tradi-tional snack, usually stuffed with potatoes or ground meat. The yoghurt in this excellent recipe adds richness to the dough and tastes wonderful with the lightly spiced filling. Samosas may be made in advance and reheated in a 350°F (180°C) preheated oven, or you can save the deep-frying until just before serving. Serve them with chutney or any of the hot relishes in the condiment section.

Pastry

All-purpose flour	2 cups (500 mL)
Salt	1 tsp (5 mL)
Butter	3 Tbsp (50 mL) melted
Yoghurt	6 Tbsp (90 mL), approximately

Filling

Ground lean lamb	1 1/4 lb (560 g)
Vegetable oil	2 Tbsp (25 mL)
Garlic	4 cloves, finely minced
Red onion	1 large, finely minced
Fresh hot green chilies	4 large, finely minced
Fresh ginger root	2-inch (5-cm) piece, peeled and finely minced
Turmeric	1 tsp (5 mL)
Cayenne	1 tsp (5 mL)
Ground cloves	1/4 tsp (1 mL)
Ground coriander	1/4 tsp (1 mL)
Ground cinnamon	1/4 tsp (1 mL)
Ground cardamon	1/4 tsp (1 mL)
Tomatoes	2, peeled and finely minced
Lemon juice	1 Tbsp (15mL)
Freshly boiled potatoes	2 cups (500 mL) diced 1/4 inch (0.5 cm)
Fresh or frozen peas	2 cups (500 mL)
Salt	1/2 tsp (2 mL)
Freshly ground pepper	1/2 tsp (2 mL)
Yoghurt	1/2 cup (125 mL), for sealing dough
Vegetable oil	for frying, to cover 1/2 inch (1 cm) in skillet

1 To make pastry, mix the flour and salt in a bowl. Drizzle with melted butter and add yoghurt by the spoonful. Blend until mixture holds together. On a lightly floured surface take small amounts of dough under the heel of your hand and slide in a streak — this mixes the dough thoroughly. Wrap the dough in plastic wrap and let rest in refrigerator for at least 2 hours.

2 For the filling, brown the lamb in a large ungreased skillet and drain thoroughly. Using the same skillet, heat vegetable oil and fry garlic, onion, chilies, and ginger. When onion is soft, stir in turmeric, cayenne, cloves, coriander, cinnamon, and cardamon and cook for 3 minutes.

3 Add tomatoes, lemon juice, potatoes and peas and season with salt and pepper. Cover and simmer for 15 minutes, or until liquid is nearly absorbed. Let cool, then refrigerate for at least 2 hours; overnight is even better.

4 To make samosas, divide dough into 10 pieces. Dust working surface with flour. Pat each piece of dough into a circle and roll into a circle at least 10 inches (25 cm) in diameter. Cut circle in half.

5 Fill one side of each half-circle with 1/4 cup (50 mL) of the cold meat filling, leaving a small border. Paint border with yoghurt, then fold over to make a triangle. Press edges to seal. Flatten slightly so they will cook evenly.

6 To cook, heat 1/2 inch (1 cm) oil in a heavy skillet until almost smoking. Add the samosas, but do not crowd. Cook for 3-5 minutes, or until golden brown on each side. Drain on paper toweling.

7 Samosas can be baked for 15 minutes at 400°F (200°C), but crust won't be tender. They can also be deep-fried. If you wish to freeze before frying, omit potatoes.

Yields 20

CHICKEN SATE

Pronounced "satay", this appetizer, usually made with chicken, pork or shrimp, is very popular throughout southeast Asia and is often sold by street vendors. The meat is marinated, threaded on skewers, and served with a spicy, peanut sauce.

Chicken breasts	4 large, skinned and boned
Soy sauce	3 Tbsp (50 mL)
Lemon juice	2 Tbsp (25 mL)
Garlic	4 cloves, crushed
Cayenne	1/4 tsp (1 mL)
Peanut oil	2 Tbsp (25 mL)

1 Lightly pound chicken breasts and cut into 3/4-inch (2-cm) squares. Combine in a bowl with soy sauce, lemon juice, garlic, and cayenne. Marinate at least 2 hours in refrigerator.

2 Thread the chicken on skewers. Brush with oil and place over hot coals or under a broiler for about 10 minutes, turning once. Serve with sate sauce (see recipe below.)

Serves 4.

Sate Sauce

Garlic	3 cloves, peeled
Shallots	3, peeled
Roasted unsalted peanuts	1 cup (250 mL)
Fresh hot chilies	3 medium
Fresh ginger root	1-inch (2.5-cm) piece, peeled and thinly sliced
Soy sauce	1 Tbsp (15 mL)
Brown sugar	2 Tbsp (25 mL)
Fresh lemon juice	juice of 1/2 lemon or 4 1/2 tsp (22 mL)
Water	1 cup (250 mL), approximately

1 Place all ingredients in a blender or food processor, and process for 2 minutes.

2 Pour the sauce into the top part of a double boiler and bring to a boil over direct heat. Place over boiling water and cook for 30 minutes, stirring occasionally.

3 Thin to desired consistency with additional water. Serve hot as a dip with sate.

SPICY NUTS

Good with drinks and very good as a garnish for soup and many vegetable dishes. Have them on standby in the refrigerator to be reheated in a 300°F (150°C) oven for five minutes before serving.

Blanched almonds or raw cashews	2 cups (500 mL)
Vegetable oil	3 Tbsp (50 mL)
Salt	1 tsp (5 mL)
Ground coriander	1/4 tsp (1 mL)
Ground cloves	pinch
Ground cinnamon	pinch
Cayenne	1 tsp (5 mL)

1 Heat a medium-sized cast iron skillet over medium heat. Add the vegetable oil and when oil is hot, add nuts. Stir and fry for 3-5 minutes until golden brown. Remove nuts and drain on paper towels.

2 Combine salt, coriander, cloves, cinnamon, and cayenne. Sprinkle over hot nuts. Mix well. Serve warm.

Yields 2 cups (500 mL)

SWEET RED PEPPER DIP

This is a hotter version of the sweet red pepper dip that was given to us by Marilyn Linton, Food Editor of *Homemaker's* magazine. Dip into it crunchy chilled vegetables, bread sticks or corn chips.

Sweet red peppers	5 large
Ripe tomatoes	4 large
Garlic	5 cloves, peeled
Ground almonds	3 1/2 oz (105 g)
Mayonnaise	1/2 cup (125 mL)
Red wine vinegar	1 Tbsp (15 mL)
Olive oil	1/4-1/2 cup (50-125 mL)
Salt	1/2 tsp (2 mL)
Freshly ground pepper	1/4 tsp (1 mL)
Cayenne	2 1/2 tsp (12 mL)

1 Broil peppers until the skins are blistered and blackened all over. Cool, then peel and seed.

2 Peel and seed tomatoes. Chop pulp coarsely and blot on paper towels.

3 Place peppers, tomatoes, garlic, almonds, mayonnaise, and red wine vinegar in a food processor or blender. Purée, slowly adding olive oil until mixture is consistency of thick sauce. Season with salt and pepper. Stir in cayenne. Chill for 3 hours to blend flavours.

Yields 3 cups (750 mL)

Clockwise: Cheese and Pepper Bread; Chili — Pepper Oil; Hot Chicken Soup with Ginger and Papaya.

COLD PORK WITH GARLIC

I like these ginger and spiced morsels best speared with a toothpick and nibbled with a light beer as an appetizer, but they are just as good as part of a sandwich that includes some rocking hot mustard.

Pork loin or rump	1 lb (450 g)
Green onions	2
Fresh ginger root	2 large slices, peeled
Salt	1 1/2 tsp (7 mL)
Soy sauce	2 Tbsp (25 mL)
Dried crushed chilies	1 tsp (5 mL)
Garlic	7 1/2 tsp (37 mL) crushed or finely chopped
Vinegar	2 tsp (10 mL)
Sugar	1 tsp (5 mL)
Vegetable oil	2 Tbsp (25 mL)
Water	1 Tbsp (15 mL)

1 Slice the green onion into long strips.

2 Place the pork in a large pot and add enough water to cover the meat. Add the green onions, ginger, and 1 tsp (5 mL) of salt. Bring to a boil and continue cooking over medium heat for 30 minutes, or until pork is tender. Remove the pork.

3 Mix together the soy sauce, remaining salt, crushed chilies, garlic, vinegar, sugar, oil, and 1 Tbsp (15 mL) of water. Let stand for 15 minutes.

4 Cut the cooled pork into very thin slices and arrange on a platter. Stir the soy sauce mixture to combine the ingredients that have settled to the bottom and pour the mixture over the pork. Serve at room temperature.

Serves 4

FRIED CHICKEN WINGS WITH SPICY DIPS

A variation (and improvement) on the chicken wings served in fast food outlets. Serve with any or all of the following sauces — mustard, plum, barbecue (see recipes below). The sauces also are good with the chicken sate in this section or with barbecued pork purchased at Chinese stores.

Egg yolks	2
Butter	3 Tbsp (50 mL) melted
Milk or water	1/2 cup (125 mL)
Salt	1/4 tsp (1 mL)
All-purpose flour	1 cup (250 mL)
Chicken wings	2 lbs (900 g)
Egg whites	2
Oil	for deep frying

1 In a bowl, beat together egg yolks, butter, milk or water, and salt. Stir in flour until barely blended. Set aside for 1 hour.

2 To disjoint chicken wings, cut through each of the two joints. Discard wing tips or reserve for the soup pot.

3 Just before serving time, beat egg whites until stiff and fold into batter. Heat oil for frying to 365°F (185°C).

4 Dip each wing piece into batter, then fry. Do not overload fryer or wings will not be crisp. Fry until nicely browned. Drain on paper towels and serve with dipping sauce.

Serves 4, or more if served as an appetizer

Mustard Sauce

Dijon mustard	3 Tbsp (50 mL)
Olive oil	2 Tbsp (25 mL)
Sugar	1 Tbsp (15 mL)
Tabasco	1/2 tsp (2 mL)

1 Combine mustard, olive oil, sugar, and Tabasco in a small bowl. Blend with a fork until oil is completely incorporated.

Yields 1/3 cups (75 mL)

Plum Sauce

Plum sauce	1/2 cup (125 mL)
Sake or dry sherry	1 Tbsp (15 mL)
Soy sauce	1 Tbsp (15 mL)
Szechuan chili sauce	1 tsp (5 mL)

1 Combine all ingredients. Serve with deep-fried or broiled chicken wings.

Yields 1/2 cup (125 mL)

Barbecue Sauce

Ketchup	1/4 cup (50 mL)
Corn syrup	1/4 cup (50 mL)
Lemon juice	2 Tbsp (25 mL)
Vegetable oil	1 Tbsp (15 mL)
Prepared mustard	2 Tbsp (25 mL)
Tabasco	1 Tbsp (15 mL)

1 Combine all ingredients in a saucepan and stir until well mixed. Serve hot with broiled chicken wings.

Yields 3/4 cup (175 mL)

HOT YAM CHIPS

Yams are to sweet potatoes what rutabagas are to turnips — cooking cousins. Use either sweet potatoes or yams for this crisp and chewy snack. The chips go very well with chile con carne and curried dishes.

Yams or sweet potatoes	2 small
Peanut oil	1 1/2 cups (375 mL)
Cayenne	1 tsp (5 mL)
Salt	1 tsp (5 mL)

1 Wash and peel the yams or sweet potatoes. Cut into 1/8-inch (2.5-mm) slices.

2 Heat oil over medium heat in a medium-sized deep pan. Test oil by adding a potato slice; when it sizzles and is cooked in 3-5 minutes, the temperature is right. Add a handful of potato slices, stir and turn slices in oil for 3-5 minutes until golden brown.

3 Remove slices from oil and drain on paper towels. Keep warm until remaining slices are cooked. Mix together cayenne and salt and sprinkle over hot potatoes. Serve with a curry or as a snack.

Serves 4

BLACK PEPPER PÂTÉ

This is a pâté with a bite, meant to make a peaceful pâté picnic in the country a little less peaceful. Serve it cold, with chunks of French bread spread with sweet butter and with a plateful of gherkins for crunch.

Chicken livers	1 lb (450 g)
Eggs	3
Ground veal	1 lb (450 g)
Bulk sausage meat	1 lb (450 g)
Salt	2 tsp (10 mL)
Garlic	4 cloves, minced
Black peppercorns	2 Tbsp (25 mL), cracked
Cognac	1/3 cup (75 mL)
Thick-sliced bacon	1 lb (450 g)

1 Purée livers in processor or blender.

2 In a large bowl, beat the eggs. Add the livers, ground veal, sausage meat, salt, garlic, cracked black peppers, and Cognac. Mix thoroughly.

3 Line the bottom and sides of a loaf pan 13″ × 4 1/2″ × 2 1/2″ (3 L) or terrine with the pork fat, reserving a few slices for the middle and the top.

4 Place half the pâté mixture in the pan, pressing down well. Place a few more of the bacon strips on top of the pâté. Cover with remaining pâté, pressing down well. Cover with remaining bacon strips. Cover pan tightly with aluminum foil.

5 Place pâté pan in a larger pan filled with enough water to come about one-third of the way up the sides of the pâté pan. Bake in a 300°F (150°C) oven for 2 hours.

6 Remove from oven and place some heavy weights on top of the foil to cause extra fat to overflow into the base pan and compress the pâté. Leave the weights on top while the pâté cools.

7 When the pâté is cool, remove the weights. Remove the pâté from the pan and peel off bacon slices. Wrap pâté in aluminum foil and refrigerate.

Serves 6-8

SOUPS

CHILI-LIME SOUP

The corn tortillas add texture to this Mexican soup. Use the richest of chicken broth to support the fine ingredients.

Rich chicken broth	3 cups (750 mL)
Fresh lime juice	1/4 cup (50 mL)
Fresh coriander	2 Tbsp (25 mL) chopped
Crushed dried red chilies	1/4 tsp (1 mL)
Pickled jalapeño peppers	2, minced
Vegetable oil	2 Tbsp (25 mL)
Corn tortillas	3, cut in thin strips
Cooked chicken	1 cup (250 mL) cut in thin strips
Scallions	2, chopped
Lime	12 paper-thin slices, unpeeled
Salt	1/4 tsp (1 mL)

1 In a pot, heat chicken broth and add the lime juice, coriander, red chilies, and jalapeño peppers. Simmer, uncovered, over low heat for 15 minutes.

2 Meanwhile, fry tortilla strips in hot oil until lightly browned and crisp. Drain on paper towels. Add tortilla strips, chicken and scallions to broth. Season with salt.

3 Serve soup with 3 slices of lime in each bowl.

Serves 4

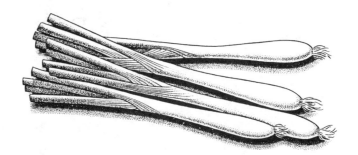

LEMON SHRIMP SOUP

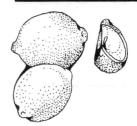

Thai food is said to be among the hottest in the world. The lemony flavours of Southeast Asian herbs are sharpened by the fresh lime juice; the heat comes from the chilies and sauces. The recipe is from the Bangkok Garden, an attractive and popular Thai restaurant in Toronto. It is described as Thailand's national soup.

Chicken broth	2 1/2 cups (625 mL)
Thai chili paste (Nam prik pan)	1 Tbsp (15 mL)
Fresh lemon grass	1 stalk, cut in 1-inch (2.5-cm) pieces
Kaffir lime leaves	2
Kha (Laos) root	2 slices
Fish sauce	1 Tbsp or to taste
Lime juice	2 Tbsp (25 mL)
Raw shrimps	12 medium, peeled and deveined
Straw mushrooms	8, cut in half
Fresh coriander	1 stalk, remove leaves, discard stalk
Fresh hot chilies	6 small, gently pounded and left whole
Scallion	1, sliced

1 Combine chicken broth and chili paste in a saucepan and bring to a boil. Add lemon grass, lime leaves, Kha root, fish sauce, and lime juice and return to the boil. Add shrimp, and as soon as the liquid returns to a boil, remove from heat; otherwise the shrimp will overcook.

2 Add the straw mushrooms, coriander leaves, chilies, and scallions. Serve immediately.

Serves 4

SHRIMP AND CUCUMBER SOUP

This is a highly spiced soup with an intense ginger taste. The dollop of yoghurt will be a welcome poultice.

Raw shrimp	1 1/2 lbs (675 g), peeled and deveined
Vegetable oil	3 Tbsp (50 mL)
Turmeric	1 tsp (5 mL)
Cucumbers	2, peeled, seeded and cubed
Onion	1, thinly sliced
Fresh hot green chilies	4, seeded and minced
Crushed dried red chilies	1/4 tsp (1 mL)
Garlic	2 cloves, finely minced
Fresh ginger root	2 Tbsp (25 mL) peeled and minced
Mustard seeds	1 Tbsp (15 mL)
Clear fish stock or chicken broth	4 cups (1 L)
Sour cream or yoghurt	4 Tbsp (60 mL)

1 In a soup pot, heat the oil over medium heat. Stir in the turmeric, cucumbers, onion, green chilies, dried chilies, garlic, ginger, and mustard seeds. Cook until vegetables are glazed, but not limp.

2 Add the shrimp on top of vegetables, cover and reduce heat. Cook over medium heat until the shrimp are firm, about 5 minutes. Pour in the fish or chicken stock and simmer for 2-3 minutes.

3 Serve in large soup plates with a spoonful of sour cream or yoghurt.

Serves 4

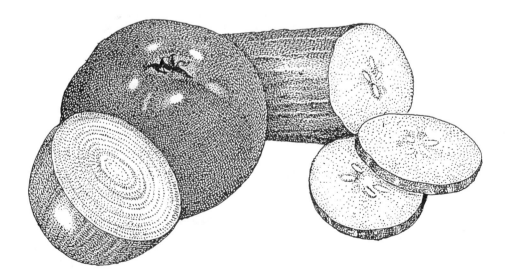

BEEF AND PEANUT SOUP WITH GREEN CHILIES

This unusual combination was even more odd before we adapted it. Originally an African recipe, it called for salt cod, as well as the peanuts and stewing beef. Now the dish is good and a bit unusual, but not shocking. Fresh hot green chilies are easily found, but taste them first; some are so mild, they're wimpy.

Stewing beef	1 lb (450 g), cut in 1-inch (2.5-cm) cubes
Water	2 cups (500 mL)
Smooth peanut butter	1 cup (250 mL)
Tomatoes	2 cups (500 mL) peeled and chopped
Onions	2 large, chopped
Fresh hot green chilies	3, seeded and diced
Crushed dried red chilies	1 tsp (5 mL)
Okra or green beans	1 lb (450 g)
Salt	1/2 tsp (2 mL) or to taste
Freshly ground pepper	1/2 tsp (2 mL) or to taste
Hard-boiled eggs	4, peeled
Green pepper	1, seeded and chopped
Onions	1, finely chopped
Hot chilies	1, finely chopped
Tomatoes	2, seeded and chopped

1 Place cubed meat and 2 cups water in a Dutch oven and simmer, covered, for 1/2 hour.

2 Add peanut butter, tomatoes, onions, green chilies, red chilies, okra or green beans to Dutch oven. Stir until peanut butter is blended. Cover and simmer for 1/2 hour, or until meat is tender. When meat is tender, season to taste with salt and freshly ground pepper.

3 Serve in large soup plates with a hard-boiled egg in the middle of each plate. Fill small bowls with chopped green peppers, onions, chilies, and tomatoes and serve as accompaniment.

Serves 4-6

TOMATO GIN SOUP

This offbeat, spicy soup is based on a recipe from Le Pavillon restaurant in Vancouver's Four Seasons Hotel.

Fresh tomatoes	5, peeled and seeded
Garlic	5 cloves, chopped
Beef stock	2 cups (500 mL)
Dried thyme	1 tsp (5 mL)
Salt	1/2 tsp (2 mL) or to taste
Freshly ground pepper	1/4 tsp (1 mL) or to taste
Bacon	4 strips
Butter	3 Tbsp (50 mL)
Fresh mushrooms	1/2 lb (225 g), sliced
Dry gin	1/3 cup (75 mL)
Tabasco	1/2 tsp (2 mL)
Whipping cream	2 cups (500 mL)

1 Put tomatoes, 3 cloves of garlic, stock, thyme, salt, and pepper in a processor. Blend to medium fine.

2 Cut the bacon into small pieces and fry until crisp.

3 Whip the butter and add the bacon, the remaining cloves of garlic and some freshly ground pepper.

4 In a soup pot, sauté the mushrooms in the butter mixture until soft.

5 Add the tomato mixture, gin, and Tabasco. Heat through; add cream just before serving.

Serves 6-8

HOT AND SOUR SOUP

This version is based on a recipe from the Mandarin restaurant in Winnipeg. The wonderful contrasts in tastes which have made this soup so popular in Chinese restaurants can easily be reproduced at home.

Dried black Chinese mushrooms	4 (available in Oriental markets)
Lean pork	2 oz (60 g)
Raw shrimps	6
Green onion	1
Eggs	2
Cornstarch	2 Tbsp (25 mL)
Water	4 Tbsp (60 mL)
White vinegar	3 Tbsp (50 mL)
Soy sauce	1 Tbsp (15 mL)
Salt	1/4 tsp (1 mL)
White pepper	1/4 tsp (1 mL)
Chicken stock	6 cups (1.5 L)
Bamboo shoots	1/4 cup (50 mL) cut into 1/4-inch (5 mm) by 1/8-inch (2.5 mm) strips
Snow peas	6, cut into 1/8-inch (2.5 mm) wide strips
Tabasco	1 tsp (5 mL)

1 Soften the mushrooms in enough hot water to cover for 30 minutes. Cut the pork across the grain in 1/4-inch (5 mm) thick slices, then cut the slices in 1/4-inch (5 mm) strips.

2 Shell and devein the shrimps. Squeeze the excess liquid from the mushrooms. Remove the stems and cut the caps into strips. Mince the green onion.

3 Beat the eggs lightly in a cup. In a second cup, combine the cornstarch and water, blending well. Combine the vinegar, soy sauce, salt and pepper in a third cup.

4 In a soup pot, bring the stock to a boil. Add the pork, bamboo shoots and mushroom strips. Bring to a boil again, then reduce heat. Skim the soup, if necessary, and add the shrimps.

5 Restir the vinegar-soy sauce mixture, add it to the soup and blend well. Stir the cornstarch mixture again and add it to the soup, stirring constantly, until the soup thickens, about 2 minutes. Add the green onions, snow pea strips and Tabasco.

6 Beat the eggs again and add it, stirring constantly, in a thin stream to form yellow threads as it sets. Serve at once.

Serves 4

MULLIGATAWNY SOUP

There are many variations on the original mulligatawny soup, which began as an Anglo-Indian soup made with beef broth, lentils, and curry powder. The name comes from the two Tamil words, *molegoo* (pepper) and *tunee* (water). I like this version, particularly if it's accompanied by steamed white rice. In India the dish is served with bananas and tomatoes.

Onion	1, diced
Carrot	1, diced
Celery	2 ribs, diced
Butter or chicken fat	1/4 cup (50 mL)
Chicken broth	4 cups (1 L)
Turmeric	1/2 tsp (2 mL)
Cayenne	2 tsp (10 mL)
Whole cloves	6
Ground coriander	1/2 tsp (2 mL)
Fresh ginger root	2 tsp (10 mL), peeled and finely minced
Bay leaf	1
Dried thyme	1/2 tsp (2 mL)
Lemon rind	1/2 tsp (2 mL) grated
Cooked chicken	1 cup (250 mL) diced
Apple	1/2 cup (125 mL) diced and peeled
Cream	1/2 cup (125 mL)
Salt	1/4 tsp (1 mL)

1 In a saucepan, sauté onion, carrot, and celery in butter or chicken fat until soft, but not browned, about 10 minutes.

2 Pour in chicken broth. Add turmeric, cayenne, cloves, coriander, ginger root, and bay leaf. Bring to a boil, reduce heat and simmer for 15 minutes.

3 Add thyme, lemon rind, chicken, and diced apple. Simmer for 15 minutes.

4 Just before serving heat cream until hot and stir cream and salt into soup.

Serves 4

SPICY GAZPACHO

This spicy liquid salad is a specialty of the Andalusia province of Spain. It is meant to be served chilled — so chilled that sometimes ice cubes are laid in the plate before the soup is poured over. It should be served with a garnish of finely chopped salad vegetables and garlic croutons.

Ripe tomatoes	3, peeled
Tomato juice	1/2 cup (125 mL)
Cucumber	1, peeled, seeded and chopped
Green pepper	1 small, seeded and chopped
Garlic	3 cloves
Dried basil	1/2 tsp (2 mL)
Ground cumin	1/4 tsp (1 mL)
Lemon juice	3 Tbsp (50 mL)
Tabasco	4 tsp (20 mL)
Olive oil	1/4 cup (50 mL)
Salt	1/2 tsp (2 mL)
Freshly ground pepper	1/2 tsp (2 mL)
Garlic croutons	1 cup (250 mL)
Fresh parsley	6 tsp (30 mL) finely chopped
Cucumber	1 small, peeled, seeded and chopped
Green pepper	1, seeded and finely chopped
Scallions	4, finely chopped
Green or ripe olives	1/2 cup (125 mL)

1 In a food processor or blender, process the tomatoes, tomato juice, cucumber, green pepper, garlic, basil, cumin, lemon juice, and Tabasco until smooth.

2 Pour into a serving bowl and stir in olive oil, salt and pepper. Chill thoroughly.

3 Fill small bowls with chopped vegetables and croutons and serve as an accompaniment.

Serves 4-6

CURRIED PEA AND LETTUCE SOUP

This is good hot or cold, but if you serve it cold, it must be very well chilled. If it's to be hot, a dollop of sour cream makes a good taste and temperature contrast.

Butter	2 Tbsp (25 mL)
Garlic	2 cloves, peeled and chopped
Onion	1 large, peeled and chopped
Turmeric	1 tsp (5 mL)
Ground cumin	1/2 tsp (2 mL)
Cayenne	1 tsp (5 mL)
Freshly ground pepper	1/2 tsp (2 mL)
Fresh ginger root	1/2 tsp (2 mL) peeled and grated
Ground coriander	1/2 tsp (2 mL)
Shelled fresh peas	4 cups (1 L)
Boston lettuce	1 head, quartered
Chicken stock	2 1/2 cups (625 mL)
Whipping cream	1 cup (250 mL)
Salt	1/2 tsp (2 mL) or to taste
Freshly ground pepper	1/2 tsp (2 mL) or to taste
Fresh chives	2 Tbsp (25 mL), for garnish
Fresh tomato	2 Tbsp (25 mL), for garnish

1 Melt the butter in a large saucepan and sauté the onion and garlic for two minutes; do not brown. Add the turmeric, cumin, cayenne, freshly ground pepper, ginger, and coriander and cook gently for two minutes. Add the peas, lettuce, and chicken broth. Simmer gently for 20 minutes.

2 Let cool and blend in a food processor or force through a sieve. Taste for seasoning and add salt and pepper.

3 Just before serving, add the cream and heat soup through without boiling. Garnish with fresh chives and chopped tomato.

Serves 4-6

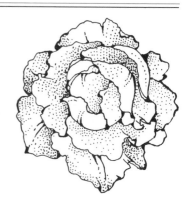

HOT CHICKEN SOUP WITH GINGER AND PAPAYA

Clear chicken broth is flavoured with fresh ginger and lime juice, then decorated with papaya for a pretty and special soup.

Chicken breasts	2 lbs (900 g)
Salt	1 tsp (5 mL)
Cayenne	2 tsp (10 mL)
Fresh lime juice	1 Tbsp (15 mL)
Chili-pepper oil	2 Tbsp (25 mL)
Onion	3/4 cup (175 mL) finely diced
Garlic	2 cloves, finely minced
Fresh ginger root	4 tsp (20 mL) peeled and minced
Chicken broth	3 cups (750 mL)
Papaya	1 small

1 Skin and bone chicken breasts and cut into bite-sized pieces. Season with salt, cayenne, and lime juice.

2 Heat oil in a saucepan and sauté onion and garlic until onion is soft. Add the chicken and ginger. Stir and cook until chicken turns white. Pour in chicken broth. Bring soup to a boil; cover. Lower heat and simmer until chicken is tender, about 10 minutes.

3 Peel and seed the papaya and cut into 1-inch (2.5-cm) pieces. Add to soup and simmer 5 minutes longer. Serve immediately.

Serves 4

BLACK BEAN SOUP

The smoothness of a hearty black bean soup is a perfect vehicle for the bite of hot chilies. This gets extra punch from the chili-wine simply made from the recipe in the condiments section. The secret to making a creamy black bean soup is to stir the beans every time you pass the stove.

Black beans	2 cups (500 mL), soaked overnight
Water	10 cups (2.5 L)
Vegetable oil	3 Tbsp (50 mL)
Onion	1, chopped
Fresh hot chilies	3, seeded and finely minced
Garlic	4 cloves, finely minced
Salt	to taste
Chili-wine	to taste
Hard-boiled eggs	2
Cooked ham	1/2 cup (125 mL) diced

1 Drain beans and place in a large saucepan with water. Bring to a boil and simmer, partially covered, for 2-3 hours, or until beans are tender and creamy.

2 Heat oil in a skillet and sauté onion, chilies, and garlic until onion is transparent. Stir into the beans and let simmer for 15 minutes.

3 Season with salt and chili-wine. Serve with slices of hard-boiled eggs and diced ham.

Serves 4-6

HOT GARLIC POTATO SOUP

A hearty and comforting soup, soothing with potatoes. Sliced tomatoes, light beer and some chewy rye bread would be good companions.

Butter	2 Tbsp (25 mL)
Onion	1 medium, diced
Garlic	6 cloves, chopped
Red pepper flakes	1 tsp (15 mL)
Potatoes	2 large, peeled and diced
Celery	1 stalk, finely chopped
Cabbage	1 cup (250 mL), diced
Chicken broth	4 cups (1 L)
Milk	1/2 cup (125 mL)
Flour	1 Tbsp (15 mL)
Sour cream	1 cup (250 mL)
Salt	1 tsp (5 mL) or to taste
Freshly ground pepper	1/2 tsp (2 mL) or to taste
Sweet red pepper	1/2, seeded and thinly sliced

1 In a soup pot, melt the butter and sauté the onion and garlic until onion is wilted. Add the red pepper flakes and sauté for 1 minute more. Add the potatoes, celery, cabbage, and chicken broth and simmer for 15 minutes, or until vegetables are tender.

2 Remove 2 cups (500 mL) of the cooked vegetables, combine with milk, flour, and sour cream and purée in a blender or food processor or mash with a fork until well blended.

3 Stir the mixture into the soup and reheat. Add salt and pepper to taste. Garnish with sweet red pepper strips and serve immediately.

Serves 6 to 8

EGGS AND CHEESE

SCRAMBLED EGGS WITH SHRIMP

Eggs always benefit from slow cooking, a requirement ensured in this recipe where the scrambled eggs are cooked in a double boiler. The resulting soft curds serve as an excellent vehicle for the spices and shrimp.

Butter	2 Tbsp (25 mL)
Scallions	4, chopped
Garlic	1 clove, minced
Sambal badjak or	1 tsp (5 mL) (available in
hot chili sauce	Oriental stores)
Green pepper	1, diced
Baby shrimps	1/2 lb (250 g) peeled and deveined
Eggs	6, lightly beaten
Whipping cream	1/4 cup (50 mL)
Salt	1/4 tsp (1 mL) or to taste
Freshly ground pepper	1/4 tsp (1 mL) or to taste

1 In the top of a large double boiler, melt the butter and sauté the scallions and garlic until soft, but do not brown. Add the sambal and green pepper; cover and cook gently over direct heat for 5 minutes. Add the shrimps and cook another two minutes.

2 Stir together the eggs and cream and pour the mixture over the shrimp mixture in the pan. Place pan over simmering water and cook, stirring continuously until eggs are scrambled, but do not overcook. Add salt and pepper.

Serves 4

SHELLFISH OMELETTE

The ingredients are combined to form a cake-like omelette in this Vietnamese dish. Serve with buttered rice as a first course or as a lunch dish.

Cooked shrimp	1 cup (250 mL)
Steamed or canned clams	1/2 cup (125 mL) drained
Scallions	1 cup (250 mL) minced
Water chestnuts	1/2 cup (125 mL) minced
Fresh ginger root	1 Tbsp (15 mL) peeled and minced
Fresh hot green chilies	4, seeded and minced
Eggs	6, lightly beaten
Peanut oil	4 Tbsp (60 mL)
Soy sauce	to taste

1   Combine all ingredients except oil and soy sauce. Heat 1 Tbsp (15 mL) oil in a skillet and spoon in 1/4 of the mixture. Cook until egg is set, then fold in half. Place in oven to keep warm. Repeat 3 more times. Serve with soy sauce.

Serves 4

SCRAMBLED EGGS WITH GINGER AND CUMIN

A dish colourful in appearance and spectacular in flavour.

Eggs	6
Milk	1/4 cup (50 mL)
Salt	1/4 tsp (1 mL)
Freshly ground pepper	1/2 tsp (2 mL)
Turmeric	1/4 tsp (1 mL)
Butter	3 Tbsp (50 mL)
Fresh ginger root	1 tsp (5 mL) peeled and finely chopped
Onions	3 Tbsp (50 mL) finely chopped
Fresh parsley	3 Tbsp (50 mL) finely chopped
Fresh hot red or green chilies	4, finely chopped
Ground cumin	1/2 tsp (2 mL)
Tomatoes	2

1 Break eggs into a bowl and mix lightly with a fork. Stir in the milk, salt, pepper, and turmeric.

2 Heat the butter in a cast iron skillet over moderate heat. Add the ginger, onions, parsley, and chilies. Fry for about one minute until onions are soft but not brown.

3 Pour in the beaten eggs and reduce heat to low. Stir eggs with a spatula until they form soft creamy curds. Do not overcook.

4 Spread the scrambled eggs on a heated serving platter and sprinkle cumin over top. Serve immediately with wedges of fresh ripe tomato.

Serves 4

CHEESE RAREBIT WITH JALAPEÑO PEPPERS

The intense taste of mustard and ale in a good rarebit is heightened here by the addition of jalapeño peppers.

Sharp Cheddar cheese	1 lb (450 g) grated
Butter	1 Tbsp (15 mL)
Ale	1 cup (250 mL)
Egg	1, lightly beaten
Dry mustard	1 tsp (5 mL)
Worcestershire sauce	2 tsp (10 mL)
Pickled jalapeño peppers	4, finely chopped
Tomatoes	2, sliced
Freshly made toast	8 slices, buttered
Bacon	4 slices, crisply cooked and crumbled

1 Melt butter in a chafing dish or in a double boiler. Add the grated cheese and stir until it melts. Very slowly add the ale, stirring constantly until thoroughly blended.

2 Mix together egg, mustard, and Worcestershire sauce. Add a few spoonfuls of hot cheese mixture. Slowly stir the egg mixture into the hot cheese. When thoroughly blended, add jalapeño peppers. Remove from heat.

3 Arrange tomato slices on the toast. Pour rarebit over and sprinkle with crumbled bacon.

Serves 4

HUEVOS RANCHEROS

The literal translation of this Mexican breakfast is ''country-style eggs'', though there's nothing calm about *this* countryside. The eggs are napped with a bright sauce of chilies and tomatoes and served on freshly fried tortillas. It's a colourful eye-opener which gives eggs — and breakfast — new meaning.

Vegetable oil	2 Tbsp (25 mL)
Onion	1 medium, finely chopped
Garlic	1 medium clove, finely minced
Ripe tomatoes	4 medium, peeled, seeded and chopped
or	
Canned Italian plum tomatoes	2 cups (500 mL) drained and chopped
Fresh or canned serrano or jalapeño peppers	2, seeded and finely chopped
Sugar	1/2 tsp (2 mL)
Fresh coriander	1 Tbsp (15 mL) finely chopped
Salt	1/4 tsp (1 mL)
Vegetable oil	1/4 cup (50 mL)
Tortillas	8, (available in specialty stores)
Butter	4 Tbsp (60 mL)
Eggs	8
Ripe avocado	1, peeled, pitted and thinly sliced
Fresh green chilies	3, seeded and finely chopped, (optional)

1 In a heavy saucepan, heat 2 Tbsp (25 mL) of vegetable oil over moderate heat. Add the onions and garlic. Cook, stirring frequently until the onions are soft and transparent, but do not brown. Stir in the tomatoes, peppers, and sugar. Bring mixture to a boil, then simmer, uncovered, stirring occasionally until sauce has thickened, about 15 minutes. Add the coriander, salt and pepper. Keep sauce warm while preparing the tortillas.

2 In a heavy skillet, heat 2 Tbsp (25 mL) of oil until very hot. Fry tortillas, one at a time, for 1-2 minutes on each side until slightly golden. Replenish oil a teaspoon (5 mL) at a time. Drain tortillas between paper towels and keep warm.

3 Over moderate heat melt 2 Tbsp (25 mL) butter in a heavy skillet. Fry the eggs slowly, four at a time, until whites are set but yolks are still soft. Repeat with remaining butter and eggs.

4 On each plate, place 2 tortillas side by side. Carefully place an egg on each tortilla. Spoon a 1-inch (2.5-cm) ring of the hot sauce around each egg and garnish with sliced avocado. Serve remaining sauce and a dish of chopped chilies on the side.

Serves 4

NEW YORK FRITTATA

Basically a big omelette with chunks of fresh vegetables, this dish, based on one from New York's Dean & DeLuca, shows what good food can come from simple ingredients. Don't try to economize by using only vegetable oil; olive oil gives flavour.

Eggs	10, lightly beaten
Salt	1/2 tsp (2 mL)
White pepper	1/4 tsp (1 mL)
Tabasco	1/2 tsp (2 mL)
Olive oil	1/4 cup (50 mL)
Vegetable oil	1/3 cup (75 mL)
Potatoes	4 large, peeled and thinly sliced
Onion	1 large, thinly sliced

1 Season eggs with salt, white pepper, and Tabasco. Combine olive and vegetable oils.

2 In a large nonstick omelette pan or two 9-inch (23-cm) frying pans, heat half the oil mixture. When hot, add the potato and onion slices. Sauté, stirring gently, until the potato slices are tender, about 10 minutes. Remove from heat and add to eggs; mix thoroughly.

3 Heat remaining oil in the same pan or pans. When hot, pour potato and egg mixture into pan, lower heat, and cover. Cook gently until mixture solidifies.

4 Use cover of pan to turn the frittata over and brown the other side, or brown under preheated broiler. Remove from pan and serve at room temperature.

Serves 4-5

BASQUE OMELETTE

A liberal interpretation of the Spanish omelette, this delicious dish includes both hot and sweet peppers, a wallop of fresh garlic, and a dash of cumin. Serve it hot with one of the spicy breads from the bread section and with a green salad.

Sweet red or green pepper	2, seeded
Olive oil	2 Tbsp (25 mL)
Fresh hot red, yellow, or green chili pepper	1 small, seeded
Bermuda onions	2 cups (500 mL) thinly sliced
Garlic	6 cloves, minced
Ripe tomatoes	1 cup (250 mL) peeled and chopped
Eggs	10
Salt	1/4 tsp (1 mL)
Freshly ground pepper	1/4 tsp (1 mL)
Ground cumin	1/4 tsp (1 mL)
Butter	3-4 Tbsp (50-60 mL)

1 Cut sweet peppers and hot chili pepper lengthwise into thin strips.

2 Heat olive oil in a saucepan and sauté peppers, chili pepper, onions, and garlic for 5 minutes. Add the tomatoes and simmer, uncovered, for 15 minutes.

3 Beat the eggs until frothy. Add salt, pepper, cumin, and 1 1/4 cups (300 mL) of the tomato sauce. Stir until combined.

4 Heat butter in a large omelette pan or seasoned cast-iron skillet. When the butter foams, pour in the egg mixture. Cook over medium heat, stirring lightly with a fork until the omelette has set on the bottom. Do not overcook; the omelette should be very moist in the centre. If you prefer a drier omelette, place under a broiler for 3 minutes.

5 When cooked, place a plate over the pan and invert the omelette onto the plate. Spoon the remaining sauce over the omelette. Serve hot or at room temperature.

Serves 4-6

CHILI AND CHEESE QUICHE

This dish has all the chic appeal of quiche with the power of flavour as well. Serve it with green salad and light beer.

All-purpose flour	1 cup (250 mL)
Salt	1/2 tsp (2 mL)
Vegetable shortening	1/3 cup (75 mL)
Butter	3 Tbsp (50 mL)
Water	2-3 Tbsp (25-50 mL)
Garlic	1 clove, minced
Onion	2 Tbsp (25 mL) minced
Canned green (güero) chilies	1/2 cup (125 mL), drained and chopped
Cheddar cheese	2 cups (500 mL) grated
Egg yolks	5, lightly beaten
Whipping cream	1 1/2 cups (375 mL)
Tabasco	2 tsp (10 mL)

1 In a bowl combine flour and salt. Cut in shortening and 1 Tbsp (15 mL) butter until it is the texture of small peas. Sprinkle with water and mix until evenly moistened. Roll out to fit a 10-inch (25-cm) quiche pan. Bake at 425°F (220°C) for 12 minutes.

2 Melt 2 Tbsp (25 mL) butter in a saucepan. Sauté garlic and onion for 2 minutes. Stir in the chilies and remove from heat. Spread chili mixture into partially baked pie shell.

3 Sprinkle cheese over chili mixture. Blend the egg yolks with the cream and Tabasco and pour over the cheese. Bake at 350°F (180°C) for 30-35 minutes, or until the custard is set. Do not overcook. Best served slightly warm.

Serves 6-8

HOT CORN SOUFFLÉ

Like any soufflé, this should be served slightly creamy in the centre. This is a rich and flavourful soufflé that needs only a green salad to make it a meal.

Yellow cornmeal	1 cup (250 mL) less 1 Tbsp (15 mL)
Whole kernel corn	1 1/2 cups (375 mL)
Milk	1 cup (250 mL)
Bacon	1/2 lb (225 g)
Eggs	6, separated
Chili powder	2 tsp (10 mL)
Salt	1 tsp (5 mL)
Freshly ground pepper	1 tsp (5 mL)
Baking powder	2 tsp (10 mL)
Fresh jalapeño peppers	6, finely chopped
Parmesan or Cheddar cheese	3/4 cup (175 mL) grated

1 Preheat oven to 375°F (190°C). Soak cornmeal and corn in the milk. Heat mixture over medium heat until barely thickened. Fry bacon until crisp, then drain and crumble into corn mixture.

2 Stir in the egg yolks, chili powder, salt and pepper, baking powder, peppers, and cheese.

3 Beat egg whites until stiff. Fold one-third of the egg whites into the corn mixture. Add the rest of the whites and combine well. Pour into a buttered 2-quart (2-L) soufflé dish or deep casserole. Bake for 35 minutes, or until slightly golden on top. Do not overbake or the texture will be dry. Serve immediately.

Serves 4

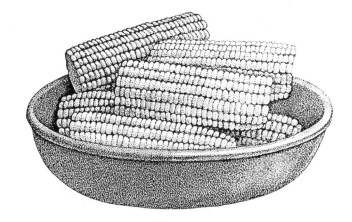

CREOLE EGGS

Softly poached eggs are napped with a spicy tomato sauce. Once the egg is broken, the yolk blends with the sauce for good contrast in spiciness and colour.

Creole sauce	1 1/2 cups (375 mL) (recipe follows)
Toast	4 slices
Eggs	4, poached

1 Heat the Creole sauce and keep warm.

2 Lay the toast on a plate and top each slice with 2 poached eggs.

3 Cover with hot Creole sauce and serve immediately.

Serves 2

Creole Sauce

Butter	1 Tbsp (15 mL)
Flour	1 Tbsp (15 mL)
Bell pepper	1, seeded and chopped
Fresh hot chili	1 small, seeded and chopped
Onion	1 medium, chopped
Fresh tomato pulp	1 1/2 cups (375 mL) chopped
Bay leaves	2
Garlic	6 cloves, chopped
Parsley	2 Tbsp (25 mL) chopped
Paprika	1 tsp (5 mL)
Salt	1/2 tsp (2 mL) or to taste

1 Melt the butter and sauté the onion, bell pepper, and chili until they become limp. Mix in the flour thoroughly.

2 Add all the remaining ingredients and season to taste with salt. Simmer slowly for 20 minutes.

FISH AND SHELLFISH

RED SNAPPER WITH SHRIMP AND GREEN OLIVES

Take care not to overcook the fish in this excellent recipe. Cooked just until the flesh begins to flake, the fish is juicy, yet intact. Use the tiny flavourful Canadian Matane shrimp from Quebec, if possible. Some specialty fish stores carry them.

Whole red snapper	3 lbs (1.5 kg), cleaned and scaled
Vegetable oil	2 Tbsp (25 mL)
Onion	1 medium, diced
Green pepper	1, seeded and diced
Carrot	1, peeled and diced
Ripe tomatoes	2 cups (500 mL) peeled and chopped
Garlic	2 cloves, finely minced
Cayenne	1 tsp (5 mL)
Fresh lemon juice	1/4 cup (50 mL)
Fresh parsley	2 Tbsp (25 mL) chopped
Salt	1/2 tsp (2 mL) or to taste
Freshly ground pepper	1/2 tsp (2 mL) or to taste
Green olives with pimento	10, halved
Fresh, tiny shrimps	1/2 cup (125 mL) shells removed

1 Heat vegetable oil in a large skillet and sauté onion, green pepper, and carrot for 10 minutes. Do not brown. Add tomatoes, garlic, and cayenne and cook over medium heat for 5 minutes. Stir in lemon juice, parsley, salt and pepper.

2 Wash red snapper under cold running water and pat dry with paper towels. Carefully lower fish into the sauce. Cover the skillet and simmer gently for about 15 minutes, or until fish is almost done. Sprinkle olives and shrimps over the fish. Cover and cook for 15 minutes.

Serves 4

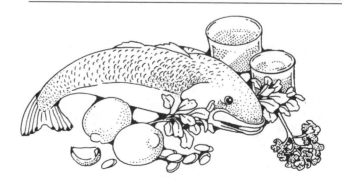

SWORDFISH KEBOBS IN YOGHURT AND GARLIC

Swordfish is used in this recipe because it is firm enough to thread reliably on skewers and remain impaled throughout the broiling, but you can use any firm white fish like halibut or haddock. The yoghurt-spice marinade makes the fish even more succulent. Serve it with steamed rice, potatoes or with an Indian bread like nan or paratha.

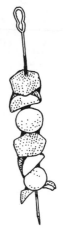

Thick fish fillets — swordfish, haddock or halibut	2 lbs (900 g), cut in 1 1/2-inch (3.5-cm) cubes
Yoghurt	1 cup (250 mL)
Garlic	3 large cloves, crushed
Cayenne	2 tsp (10 mL)
Paprika	1 tsp (5 mL)
Curry powder	1 Tbsp (15 mL)
Salt	1 tsp (5 mL)
Vegetable oil	1/4 cup (50 mL)

1 Arrange cubed fish in a shallow dish. Mix yoghurt, garlic, cayenne, paprika, curry powder, and salt. Pour over fish and cover with plastic wrap. Marinate fish for 2 hours in the refrigerator.

2 Thread cubes of fish on skewers. Spoon marinade over skewered fish, drizzle with oil and broil or grill until done, about 10-15 minutes. Do not overcook.

Serves 4

HALIBUT WITH GARLIC AND LEMON

This is a simple recipe that is good barbecued or broiled. Serve with steamed rice, Greek olives, and a green salad.

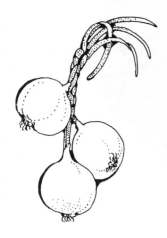

Fresh lemon juice	1/2 cup (125 mL)
Olive oil	1/2 cup (125 mL)
Garlic	10 cloves, crushed
Fresh parsley	1 Tbsp (15 mL) finely minced
Cayenne	1 tsp (5 mL)
Turmeric	big pinch
Fresh halibut	2 lb (900 g), cubed

1 Arrange cubes of fish in a shallow dish. Combine the rest of the ingredients and pour over the fish. Cover tightly with plastic wrap and marinate for 2 hours in the refrigerator. Turn fish several times during this time.

2 Remove fish from marinade and broil until brown — about 3-5 minutes on each side — do not overcook.

Serves 4

FISH ANTICUCHOS (PERUVIAN BROILED FISH)

Firm-fleshed fish is as amenable to skewer barbecuing as is meat, so don't overlook this excellent way of cooking it. The fish is marinated in spices and vinegar, threaded on wooden skewers and barbecued. To add a Peruvian touch, serve with potatoes and a spicy chili sauce.

Thick fish fillets	1-1 1/2 lbs (450-675g), cut in 1 1/2-inch (3.5-cm) cubes
Red wine vinegar	1/2 cup (125 mL)
Hot chili powder	2 tsp (10 mL)
Vegetable oil	2 Tbsp (25 mL)
Garlic	3 large cloves, finely minced
Ground cumin	1/2 tsp (2 mL)
Salt	1/2 tsp (2 mL) or to taste
Freshly ground pepper	1/2 tsp (2 mL) or to taste

1 Marinate cubed fish in mixture of vinegar, chili powder, oil, garlic and cumin for 1 hour. There's not a great deal of marinade, just enough to lightly coat cubes. Drain fish and season with salt and freshly ground pepper.

2 Thread fish on wooden or metal skewers. Broil for 10-15 minutes, or until fish is cooked. Baste with marinade during broiling.

Serves 4

SHRIMP WITH
GINGER AND CHILI SAUCE

The combination of the fresh ginger, hot chili and sake is terrific with the crunch of properly cooked shrimp. Serve with warm sake and steamed rice.

Raw shrimp	32 medium (about 2 1/2 lb or 1.25 kg)
Vegetable oil	4 Tbsp (60 mL)
Scallions	2, chopped
Garlic	2 cloves, finely minced
Fresh ginger root	1/2-inch (1-cm) slice, peeled and finely minced
Hot chili sauce	1 tsp (5 mL) (from Oriental specialty stores)
Rice wine (sake)	2 tsp (10 mL)
Spanish onion	1 small, sliced
Sugar	2 Tbsp (25 mL)
Ketchup	2 Tbsp (25 mL)
Soy sauce	2 tsp (10 mL)

1 Peel and devein shrimp. Set aside.

2 Heat oil in a wok or skillet until almost smoking. Toss in scallions, garlic, and ginger. Stir-fry for 30 seconds, then add shrimp, chili sauce, and wine. Reduce heat slightly and stir-fry until shrimps are pink.

3 Add the Spanish onion. Stir-fry for 2 minutes, then add sugar, ketchup, and soy sauce. Continue stir-frying until sauce is thick and clings to onions and shrimp, about 2 minutes.

Serves 4

Lobster with Green Chilies, Tomatoes, and Lime

SHRIMP WITH CHARRED RED PEPPERS

The shrimps are marinated in rice wine and soy sauce, then stir-fried with charred chili peppers, ginger, and garlic. The result is a dish of delicious contrasts in taste and texture.

Raw shrimps	1 lb (450 g)
Cornstarch	5 tsp (25 mL)
Egg white	1
Rice wine (sake)	4 1/2 tsp (22 mL)
Soy sauce	2 Tbsp (25 mL)
Vinegar	2 tsp (10 mL)
Sugar	1 tsp (5 mL)
Salt	1/2 tsp (2 mL)
Freshly ground pepper	1/2 tsp (2 mL)
Peanut oil	4 Tbsp (60 mL)
Dried red chili peppers	8
Green onion	4 1/2 tsp (22 mL) finely chopped
Fresh ginger root	2 tsp (10 mL) peeled and finely chopped
Garlic	2 tsp (10 mL) finely chopped

1 Shell and devein the shrimps. Wash well in cold water.

2 Make a marinade by mixing 2 tsp (10 mL) of the cornstarch with 2 Tbsp (25 mL) water, then beating in the egg white. Mix with the shrimps and let stand for at least 30 minutes.

3 In a bowl, mix together the remaining cornstarch with 2 Tbsp (25 mL) water, then add the rice wine, soy sauce, vinegar, sugar, salt, and pepper. Set aside.

4 Heat oil in wok over high heat. Add the chili peppers and fry until the peppers start to turn black. (It's best to open the windows or turn on a fan, as the peppers smoke while charring.) Add the green onions, ginger, and garlic. Stir-fry briefly, but don't burn. By now the red peppers should be completely black.

5 Drain the excess marinade from the shrimps and add shrimps to the wok. Stir-fry for a few seconds until the shrimps curl. Give the bowl of pre-mixed sauce a stir and add to the wok. Stir everything together until the sauce begins to thicken and cling to the shrimps. Remove immediately to a serving dish and serve with rice.

Serves 4

LOBSTER WITH GREEN CHILIES, TOMATOES, AND LIME

This recipes uses a cross-cultural combination of spices to create a colourfully spicy lobster dish. The lime-chili combination is Mexican, and the turmeric gives it an Indian touch. Use the freshest possible lobsters. If you are loathe to execute the lobsters yourself, have it done at the market as near to cooking time as possible. Please use fresh lime juice.

Lobsters	2 1 1/2-lb (675 g)
Onions	3 large, chopped
Butter	1 cup (250 mL)
Turmeric	1 1/2 tsp (7 mL)
Fresh hot green chilies	4, seeded and finely chopped
Italian plum tomatoes	2 cups (500 mL) peeled
Salt	1 tsp (5 mL)
Fresh lime juice	4 Tbsp (60 mL)

1 If the lobsters are alive, sever the vein at the base of the neck with a sharp knife. Cut off and crack the claws. Divide the body at the tail and cut the tail into 3 or 4 pieces at the segmentations. Cut the shell in half lengthwise. Remove and discard the sac near the head and the intestinal vein that runs through the middle of the underside of the tail.

2 In a large skillet, sauté the onions in butter until translucent. Add the turmeric, green chilies, and tomatoes. Simmer, uncovered, for 5 minutes.

3 Add the lobster to the skillet, cover and cook about 7 minutes. Add the salt and lime juice. Do not boil, as boiling can create a sour taste. Serve with rice or hot buttered noodles.

Serves 4

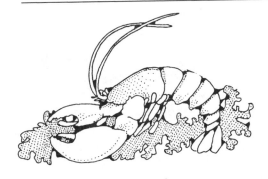

HOT PAELLA

The methods of preparing a traditional Spanish paella vary widely. Some paellas call just for meat, others for seafood, still others for a combination. A traditional paella has some spiciness to it, usually only provided by the biting chorizo sausage. This recipe takes it one step further with the addition of extra garlic and a shot of hot chili sauce. The recipe may be adjusted to larger or smaller numbers, providing that you allow double volume of liquid to rice, so the paella will not be too dry. Allow about 1/2 cup (125 mL) of rice per person. Traditionally, the dish is served in the large, shallow pan in which it is cooked.

Frying chicken	3 lb (1.5 kg), cut into serving pieces
Olive oil	1/2 cup (125 mL)
Garlic	4 cloves, finely minced
Onions	2 large, sliced
Sweet red pepper	1, seeded and cut into 1/2-inch (1-cm) strips
Long-grain rice	2 cups (500 mL)
Chicken or clam broth	3 cups (750 mL)
Tomato sauce	1 cup (250 mL)
Saffron threads	1/2 tsp (2 mL)
Salt	1 tsp (5 mL)
Freshly ground pepper	1 tsp (5 mL)
Hot chili sauce	3 Tbsp (50 mL) (from Oriental specialty stores)
Pepper wine or dry sherry	2 Tbsp (25 mL)
Raw shrimp	1 lb (500 g)
Clams in shell	20 large
Chorizo sausage	1 lb (450 g), cut into 1/2-inch (1-cm) pieces
Fresh or frozen peas	1 cup (250 mL)
Tomatoes	4, peeled and quartered
Capers	1/2 cup (125 mL)

1 Peel the shrimp and remove the black vein that runs along the back. Scrub clams with a wet vegetable brush to remove any grit on the shells.

2 Sauté the chicken pieces in the olive oil, over medium heat until golden brown. Remove chicken and set aside. Add the garlic, onions, and red pepper and cook over low heat until the onion is translucent. Add the rice and sauté until golden.

3 Pour in chicken or clam broth, tomato sauce, saffron, salt and freshly ground pepper. Bring to a boil, cover and simmer for 10 minutes until rice is partially cooked. Stir in chili sauce and pepper wine.

4 In a large casserole or 2 smaller ones, or a paella pan, put half the shrimp, clams, chorizo, peas, tomatoes, and capers. Top this with about 3/4 of the rice mixture. Arrange the chicken pieces, the rest of the shellfish, chorizo, tomatoes, peas, and capers on top of rice. Spoon remaining rice mixture over this. Cover the casserole and bake at 325°F (160°C) for 30-45 minutes until rice is tender. Check once during cooking, and if paella seems too dry, add a little broth or water. Remove cover and bake for 5 minutes until rice is fluffy.

Serves 4

PERUVIAN MARINATED SHRIMP

Though fish is often left raw for Peruvian ceviches, in this dish the shrimp are very lightly cooked first. In Peru the dish is often served cold, with hot, sweet potatoes and chunks of corn on the cob.

Raw shrimp	2 lbs (900 g)
Scallions	4, thinly sliced
Lemon juice	1/2 cup (125 mL)
Fresh hot chilies	4 small, seeded and finely minced
Chili-pepper oil or olive oil	1/4 cup (50 mL)
Fresh parsley	2 Tbsp (25 mL) finely chopped
Freshly ground pepper	1/2 tsp (2 mL) or to taste
Salt	1/2 tsp (2 mL) or to taste

1 Boil the whole shrimp in water for 2 minutes. Let cool. Peel and remove the black vein that runs along the back.

2 Place the shrimp in a bowl. Add the scallions, lemon juice, chilies, oil, parsley, salt and pepper to taste. Stir gently to combine. Marinate for 1 hour in the refrigerator, stirring several times.

Serves 4

KIM MURRELL'S SHRIMP CREOLE

Generally Creole dishes differ from Cajun, in that Creole food is thought to be more urban than the rural-based Cajun. But the dishes are often so similar that some experts take the easy road and call them both "Louisiana cooking." This excellent example of "Louisiana cooking" was contributed by Kim Murrell of the Privateer's Warehouse restaurant in Halifax, who spent many years in Louisiana.

Bacon	1 1/4 cups (300 mL), diced
Onion	1 cup (250 mL), finely chopped
Celery	1 cup (250 mL), julienne cut
Green pepper	3/4 cup (175 mL) diced
Garlic	1 Tbsp (15 mL) chopped
Dried thyme	3/4 tsp (3 mL), crumbled
Dried sweet basil	1 tsp (5 mL)
Dried oregano	1/2 tsp (2 mL)
Cayenne	2 tsp (10 mL)
Tomatoes	2 cups (500 mL), peeled, seeded and chopped
Tomato sauce	3/4 cup (175 mL)
Sugar	1 Tbsp (15 mL)
Raw shrimps	36 medium, shelled and deveined

1 Sauté bacon to render fat. Remove and reserve bacon bits. Add onion, celery, and green pepper and sauté until soft.

2 Add garlic, thyme, basil, oregano, and cayenne. Cook 2 minutes.

3 Add the tomatoes, tomato sauce, and sugar. Simmer for 1 1/2 hours, stirring occasionally.

4 Add shrimps and cook for 5-7 minutes until shrimps are cooked. Serve over hot rice and garnish with lots of crisp bacon.

Serves 4-6

FRESH OYSTERS IN
HOT CHILI SAUCE

This dish is unusual, though the combination of flavours shouldn't be too startling. Raw oysters often are served with a very spicy tomato-based sauce as a condiment. In this recipe, the oysters are lightly cooked in a hot sauce spiked with garlic. It is an excellent first course or late night snack served with garlic toast and chilled beer.

Fresh, raw oysters	4 cups (1 L) drained
Chili-pepper or olive oil	3 Tbsp (50 mL)
Garlic	4 cloves, finely minced
Tomato paste	1/2 cup (125 mL)
Clam, oyster or chicken broth	1 1/2 cups (375 mL)
Hot chili sauce	1 Tbsp (15 mL)
Pepper-wine or dry sherry	2 Tbsp (25 mL)
Dried oregano	1 tsp (5 mL)
Fresh parsley	1 Tbsp (15 mL), finely minced
Salt	1/2 tsp (2 mL) or to taste
Freshly ground pepper	1/2 tsp (2 mL) or to taste

1 In a saucepan, heat oil and sauté garlic until golden, but do not brown. Stir in tomato paste, broth, chili sauce, pepper-wine or dry sherry, oregano, and parsley. Stir until thoroughly blended and hot.

2 Add the fresh oysters. When oysters begin to curl around the edges, the dish is cooked. Season to taste with salt and freshly ground pepper. Serve immediately.

Serves 4

MALAYSIAN MUSSELS OLÉ MALACCA

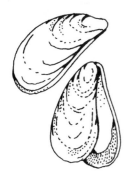

This is deservedly one of the most popular dishes at the Olé Malacca Malaysian restaurant in Toronto. Mussels are cooked in their shell and served covered in a wonderfully spicy, dense chili-egg sauce. You must pick the shells out of the sauce with your fingers. The dish should probably be eaten in the bathtub.

Fresh ginger root	2 1/4-inch (5-mm) slices, peeled
Garlic	2 large cloves
Fresh hot red chilies	4
Black soya beans	1 Tbsp (15 mL) (from Oriental specialty stores)
Hot sambal	1 Tbsp (15 mL) (from Oriental specialty stores)
Vegetable oil	4 Tbsp (60 mL)
Mussels	16 large
Eggs	2, lightly beaten
Roasted unsalted peanuts	3 Tbsp (50 mL)
Tomato ketchup	2 Tbsp (25 mL)
Sugar	2 tsp (10 mL)
Salt	1 tsp (5 mL)
Scallions	2, finely sliced

1 To make the rempah (sauce base), pound together ginger, garlic, chilies, soya beans, and sambal.

2 Scrub mussels with a brush and remove with a firm yank the hairy "beard" attached to the edge.

3 Heat a large skillet until hot and pour in oil. Stir-fry the rempah for 2 minutes, then add the mussels. Pour the eggs over the mussels and quickly add peanuts, ketchup, sugar, and salt. Stir-fry until egg is done and mussels have opened. Serve immediately, garnished with sliced scallions.

Serves 2

GINGERED CRABMEAT
SAUCE WITH GREEN PEAS

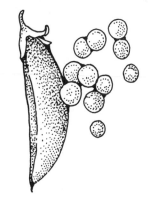

This attractive dish has lots of spicy ginger sauce; it should be served with enough rice so the sauce has a vehicle. With the ingredients assembled, it can be cooked in 10 minutes.

Fresh peas	2 lbs (900 g) unshelled, or
	2 cups (500 mL) shelled
Water	1 1/2 cups (625 mL)
Peanut oil	3 Tbsp (50 mL)
Scallions	4, minced
Fresh ginger root	1 Tbsp (15 mL) peeled and grated
Fresh hot chilies	4, thinly sliced lengthwise
or	
Szechuan chili sauce	2 tsp (10 mL)
Fresh or frozen crabmeat	1 cup (250 mL)
Dry sherry or chili-wine	1 Tbsp (15 mL)
Chicken stock	1 cup (250 mL)
Cornstarch	1 Tbsp (15 mL)
Water	2 Tbsp (25 mL)

1 Parboil peas in 1 1/2 cups (675 mL) water for 1 minute. Drain and set aside.

2 Heat a wok or large skillet over high heat until hot. Add the oil and heat until hot, but not smoking. Lower heat slightly, add the scallions, ginger, and chilies. Stir-fry for 20 seconds.

3 Add the crabmeat, sherry or chili-wine, and the peas. Mix well. Pour in the chicken stock. Cover and steam vigorously for 1 minute.

4 Meanwhile, blend together the cornstarch and 2 Tbsp (25 mL) water. Add to peas and stir briskly until sauce is smooth and thick. Pour into a hot serving dish.

Serves 4

KEN MURRELL'S MARITIME BOUILLABAISSE

This delicious bouillabaisse recipe comes from Privateer's Warehouse restaurant in Halifax, Nova Scotia. It will take time to assemble the ingredients and blend their flavours, but it's well worth it. The soup is served with rouille, a mayonnaise-like sauce, spicy with garlic and chilies.

Olive oil	1/3 cup (75 mL)
Onion	2 cups (500 mL) julienne cut
Fresh fennel	1/2 cup (125 mL) julienne cut
Leek	1/2 cup (125 mL) julienne cut
Garlic	3 cloves, chopped
Dried thyme	1/2 tsp (2 mL)
Dried sweet basil	1/4 tsp (1 mL)
Bay leaf	1
Tomatoes	6 cups (1.5 L) peeled, seeded and chopped
Dry white wine	2 cups (500 mL)
Water	6 cups (1.5 L)
Fish heads, bones, trimmings	2 lbs (900 g)
Orange peel	3-inch (7.5-cm) piece, julienne cut
Saffron threads	1 tsp (5 mL) crumbled
Lobsters	2 1-lb (450-g), cut up and claws cracked
Salmon fillet	12 oz (350 g), cut in large pieces
Haddock fillet	12 oz (350 g), cut in large pieces
Raw shrimps	12 medium, shelled and deveined
Scallops	12
Clams in shell	18, scrubbed
Mussels in shell	18, bearded and scrubbed
Pernod	1 1/2 oz (40 mL)

1 Heat olive oil in a Dutch oven. When oil is hot, add the onion, fennel, leek, garlic, thyme, basil, and bay leaf. Do not brown.

2 Add tomatoes to the Dutch oven and cook for 5 minutes. Pour in wine, water, and fish trimmings (tied in cheesecloth), orange peel, and saffron. Quickly bring to a boil, reduce heat and simmer, uncovered, for 30 minutes.

3 Remove and discard the fish trimmings. Bring broth to a boil. Add the lobster and boil for 3 minutes. Reduce heat and add the salmon and haddock. Simmer for 5-7 minutes.

4 Add the shrimps, scallops, clams and mussels. Simmer for 5-7 minutes; now add Pernod.

5   Remove the seafood from the soup with a slotted spoon and keep on a heated platter. Place the soup in a large soup tureen.

6   At the table, place a freshly-made piece of buttered toast (French bread) in each soup bowl, ladle soup over bread and arrange seafood on top. Serve with a hearty dollop of rouille sauce (recipe follows).

Serves 6-8 generously

Rouille Sauce

Green peppers	2 small
Fresh hot chili pepper	1 medium, seeded and chopped
or	
Tabasco	to taste
Water	1 cup
Pimentos	2, drained and dried
Garlic	4 cloves, chopped
Olive oil	6 Tbsp (90 mL)
Fine dry breadcrumbs	1-3 Tbsp (15-50 mL)

1   Preheat broiler and broil green peppers until skin is blistered on all sides. Rinse peppers under cool water and peel and seed.

2   Combine all ingredients except the breadcrumbs and Tabasco and process on low speed in a blender or food processor.

3   Remove from the blender and add enough bread crumbs so that sauce will hold its shape. Add Tabasco now if chili pepper was omitted.

4   Before serving, thin with 3 Tbsp (50 mL) of bouillabaisse broth.

CREOLE CRAB GUMBO

To qualify as a gumbo, a dish must have okra as its principal ingredient. The word "gumbo" is, in fact, Creole patois for the African word for okra. In this hearty dish the crabmeat is added right at the end of the cooking, after the tomatoes, onion, garlic, and spices have simmered and blended. Serve the gumbo over rice in big bowls.

Bacon	1 cup (250 mL) diced
Butter	4 Tbsp (60 mL)
Onion	1/2 cup (125 mL) chopped
Okra	2 cups (500 mL) sliced
Tomatoes	1 1/2 cups (375 mL) peeled and chopped
Tomato juice	1 cup (250 mL)
Garlic	3 cloves, finely chopped
Lemon	2 slices
Bay leaf	2
Water	1 cup (250 mL)
Salt	1/2 tsp (2 mL)
Cayenne	2 tsp (10 mL)
Flour	1 Tbsp (15 mL)
Filé powder	1 tsp (5 mL)
Butter	1 Tbsp (15 mL)
Fresh or frozen crabmeat	2 cups (500 mL)

1 In a large saucepan, fry the bacon over medium heat until it begins to brown. Add 2 Tbsp (25 mL) butter and onion and cook for 5 minutes, stirring frequently.

2 Add the okra, tomatoes, tomato juice, garlic, lemon slices, bay leaf, water, salt, and cayenne. Simmer, partially covered, for 45 minutes.

3 Blend together the flour, filé powder, and remaining butter. Add to tomato mixture, stirring continuously. When thickened, add the crabmeat.

Serves 4

CHICKEN AND DUCK

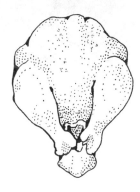

CHILI-PEPPER CHICKEN

A wok dish of chicken cubes in a light coating, with a sherry-cider vinegar sauce. Serve with steamed rice and a green vegetable.

Chicken breasts	6 halves, skinned and boned
Salt	1/2 tsp (2 mL)
Szechuan peppercorns	1/2 tsp (2 mL)
Egg white	1, well-beaten
Cornstarch	1 Tbsp (15 mL)
Whole dried chili peppers	8
Fresh ginger root	1 Tbsp (15 mL), peeled and minced
Scallions	3, finely chopped
Sugar	1 Tbsp (15 mL)
Salt	1/4 tsp (1 mL)
Cider vinegar	2 Tbsp (25 mL)
Soy sauce	2 Tbsp (25 mL)
Dry sherry	1 Tbsp (15 mL)
Sesame oil	2 tsp (10 mL)
Peanut oil	2 cups (500 mL)

1 In a small skillet, heat peppercorns until fragrant. Crush warm peppercorns in a mortar and pestle.

2 Cut the chicken into cubes and place in a bowl. Mix in the salt, Szechuan peppercorns, egg white, and cornstarch and let sit for 15 minutes.

3 Arrange chili peppers, ginger, and scallions on a plate. Make sauce by mixing together sugar, salt, cider vinegar, soy sauce, sherry, and sesame oil.

4 Heat peanut oil in a wok or large skillet until hot, 375°F (190°C). Fry chicken cubes until golden brown, stirring constantly so they don't stick. Remove chicken and drain. Strain the oil through a sieve into a bowl.

5 Return 2 Tbsp (25 mL) oil to the wok and heat over medium heat. Scatter in the chili peppers and stir-fry until they darken. Increase heat and stir-fry the ginger and scallions. Return chicken to wok. Pour in the sauce and stir until the chicken is well coated.

Serves 4

CHICKEN WITH ORANGE AND CHILIES

This is a rightly popular dish in Szechuan restaurants that can be easily and satisfactorily prepared at home. Note the marinating and baking times — the chicken is marinated for 2 hours and the orange peel is baked for 2 hours before they are combined with the other ingredients.

Oranges	3
Boned white chicken meat	2 lbs (900 g)
Egg whites	2
Soy sauce	4 tsp (20 mL)
Cornstarch	1 tsp (5 mL)
Peanut oil	3 Tbsp (50 mL)
Scallions	2, finely chopped
Fresh ginger root	1 Tbsp (15 mL) peeled and minced
Whole dried chili peppers	20
Chicken stock	1 Tbsp (15 mL)
White sugar	7 tsp (35 mL)
Liquid honey	1 Tbsp (15 mL)

1 Peel the zest from the oranges and cut into 3/4-inch (2-cm) squares. Place the orange peel pieces in a 200°F (95°C) oven for about 2 hours, or until they are dry and begin to crisp. Remove from the oven.

2 Cut the chicken into 3/4-inch (2-cm) cubes. Combine with the egg whites, 1 tsp (5 mL) soy sauce, and cornstarch until well coated. Marinate for 2 hours, stirring occasionally.

3 Heat a wok until hot, then pour in peanut oil. Add the chicken and stir-fry for 3 minutes, or until golden brown. Remove chicken from wok.

4 Stir-fry the scallions and ginger for 1 1/2 minutes.

5 Return chicken to wok, along with the chili peppers, orange peel, chicken stock, sugar, honey and 3 tsp (15 mL) soy sauce. Stir-fry this mixture for about 2 minutes. Watch carefully that it doesn't burn.

6 Serve over hot rice.

Serves 4

PEPPERCORN CHICKEN

Szechuan peppercorns are sold whole and seeded. Buy the seeded because most of the flavour comes from the husks anyway. Serve this spicy dish hot or cold. In summer cook it on the barbecue. Note that the chicken marinates in the spices for at least a day before it is cooked.

Salt	1 Tbsp (15 mL)
Szechuan peppercorns	1 tsp (5 mL)
Cracked black peppercorns	1 tsp (5 mL)
Crushed dried hot chilies	1 tsp (5 mL)
Whole chicken	3 lb (1.5 kg), quartered

1 In a small skillet, toast the salt, Szechuan peppercorns, black peppercorns, and crushed chilies until salt turns light brown. Shake the skillet occasionally.

2 Grind salt and peppercorn mixture in a mortar and pestle or coffee grinder until fine. Rub mixture over chicken quarters. Place in a glass or enamel dish, cover tightly with plastic wrap and refrigerate for 1-2 days.

3 Place chicken, skin side up, on a rack in a roasting pan. Cover and bake at 300°F (150°C) for 45 minutes to 1 hour. Remove cover and slip under the broiler until skin is lightly browned.

Serves 4

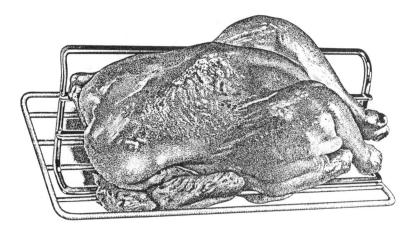

PEPPER CHICKEN SALAD

A salad crunchy with Romaine, hot with fresh ginger and roasted Szechuan peppercorns.

Cooked chicken	4 cups (1 L), 1 1/2-inch (4-cm) strips
Romaine lettuce	4 cups (1 L) shredded
Scallions	3, finely minced
Fresh ginger root	1-inch (2.5-cm) piece, peeled and finely minced
Szechuan peppercorns	2 tsp (10 mL) crushed
Soy sauce	4 Tbsp (60 mL)
Cider vinegar	4 tsp (20 mL)
Sugar	1 tsp (5 mL)
Cayenne	1 tsp (5 mL)
Peanut oil	1 Tbsp (15 mL)

1 Toss the chicken and lettuce together in a large bowl. Toast the peppercorns in a small skillet over medium heat for a few minutes until they become fragrant.

2 To make dressing, pound the scallions, ginger, and peppercorns in a mortar and pestle. Add the soy sauce, cider vinegar, sugar, cayenne, and oil. Blend thoroughly and pour over the chicken and lettuce. Toss until evenly coated.

Serves 4 as a main dish or 8-10 as an appetizer

TANDOORI CHICKEN

In this classical East Indian dish the chicken is marinated in yoghurt and spices, then is traditionally baked vertically in a clay oven called a *tandoor*. However, this recipe is designed for a standard oven.

Chicken	3-4 lbs (1.5-2 kg)
Fresh ground pepper	1 tsp (5 mL)
Cayenne	1 Tbsp (15 mL)
Fresh lemon juice	4 Tbsp (50 mL)
Onions	2 medium, chopped
Fresh ginger root	3-inch (7.5-cm) piece, peeled and chopped
Garlic	6 large cloves, peeled
Whole coriander seeds	2 tsp (10 mL)
Whole cumin seeds	1 Tbsp (15 mL)
Cayenne	1 Tbsp (15 mL)
Yoghurt	1 cup (250 mL)
Butter	2 Tbsp (25 mL)

1 Quarter the chicken, remove the skin and rub with pepper, cayenne and 2 Tbsp (25 mL) lemon juice. Set aside while making marinade.

2 In a food processor or blender, process onions, ginger, garlic, coriander, cumin seeds, 2 Tbsp (25 mL) lemon juice, cayenne, and yoghurt until it makes a smooth paste.

3 Place chicken in a bowl and coat with yoghurt mixture. Cover and refrigerate for at least 3 hours, or overnight, if possible.

4 Place chicken in a baking pan and dot with butter. Bake, uncovered, at 450°F (230°C) for 1 hour. Baste occasionally with pan juices.

Serves 4

CHICKEN IN RED CURRY

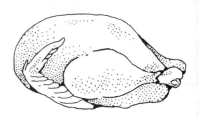

This terrific curry gets its colour from red chilies and its special flavour from freshly-made coconut milk.

Chicken breasts	4 halves
Crushed dried red chilies	1/4 cup (50 mL)
Coriander seeds	1/2 tsp (2 mL)
Cumin seeds	big pinch
Mace	big pinch
Ground nutmeg	big pinch
Scallions	2, minced
Garlic	5 large cloves, minced
Lemon zest	1/4 tsp (1 mL), minced
Fresh parsley	1 Tbsp (15 mL) finely chopped
Vinegar	1 Tbsp (15 mL)
Coconut milk	3 cups (750 mL) (see recipe below)
Salt	to taste

1 Remove skin and bones from chicken breasts and cut meat into 1/2-inch (1-cm) strips.

2 To make red curry paste, lightly toast the chilies, coriander, cumin, mace, and nutmeg in a small skillet. Blend or crush in a mortar and pestle until coarsely ground. Mix with the scallions, garlic, lemon zest, parsley, and vinegar.

3 In a skillet, boil 1 cup (250 mL) of the coconut milk until reduced by half. Stir in red curry paste and simmer for 2 minutes. Add the chicken and sauté until done, about 2 minutes. Remove chicken to a bowl.

4 Pour in remaining coconut milk and simmer for about 10 minutes, or until sauce begins to thicken. Season with salt to taste. Return chicken and cook until heated thoroughly. Serve immediately with hot rice, and, if you wish, garnish with minced scallions.

Serves 4

Quick Coconut Milk

Dessicated unsweetened coconut	4 cups (1 L)
Milk	4 cups (1 L), scalded

1 Place half the coconut in a blender and pour over 2 cups (500 mL) of the hot milk. Blend at high speed for 2 minutes. Set aside and repeat with remaining coconut and milk. Let sit until cool, then drain coconut through several thicknesses of cheesecloth. Squeeze coconut meat until dry to extract the maximum amount of liquid.

Yields 3 cups (750 mL)

CHICKEN AND PEANUT STEW

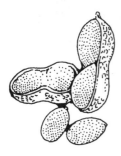

An attractive, African-style dish of chicken cooked with peanuts and chilies and served over rice, with colorful condiments.

Whole chicken	3 lb (1.5 kg), cut up
Lemon juice	1/4 cup (50 mL)
Salt	1/2 tsp (2 mL)
Flour	1 Tbsp (15 mL)
Peanut oil	2 Tbsp (25 mL)
Onions	2, chopped
Fresh ginger root	2-inch (5-cm) piece, peeled and finely minced
Chicken broth	1 1/2 cups (375 mL)
Peanut butter	3/4 cup (175 mL)
Tomato paste	2 Tbsp (25 mL)
Fresh hot red chilies	4, finely minced
Avocado	1, peeled and diced
Hard-boiled egg	1, chopped
Fresh pineapple	1/2, peeled, cored and diced
Onion	1, finely diced
Tomatoes	2, seeded and diced

1 Place chicken in a bowl and add lemon juice, mixing to coat evenly. Cover and marinate for 2 hours. Remove chicken and pat dry. Sprinkle with salt and dust with flour.

2 Heat oil in a skillet and brown chicken thoroughly. Remove chicken and sauté onion and ginger for 2 minutes. Drain excess oil from skillet.

3 Return chicken pieces to skillet. Combine chicken broth, peanut butter, tomato paste and chilies. Pour over chicken and stir to mix thoroughly. Cover and simmer for 40 minutes. Serve with hot rice and garnishes of avocado, egg, pineapple, onion, and tomato.

Serves 4

CHICKEN KIEV WITH A KICK

In a traditional Chicken Kiev, a wedge of herbed butter is rolled into the meat, which is then sealed with breadcrumbs and fried. On the first slice, the centre is released, producing a spurt of herbs and butter. In this recipe the principle is the same, but now the centre is a buttery Vesuvius of cayenne and cumin, and the outside crunches with coconut. We find one half breast per person adequate, but increase it for heartier appetites. Serve it with steamed rice, green salad and crisp chilled white wine.

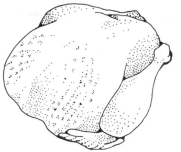

Chicken breasts	4 halves, skinned and boned
Chilled butter	4 2-inch × 1/2-inch (5-cm × 1.25-cm) pieces
Garlic	2 cloves, finely minced
Cayenne	1 Tbsp (15 mL)
Fresh parsley	1 Tbsp (15 mL) finely minced
Scallions	2, finely chopped
Ground cumin	1/2 tsp (2 mL)
Salt	1/4 tsp (1 mL)
Eggs	2, lightly beaten
Flour	1/4 cup (50 mL)
Dessicated unsweetened coconut	1 1/2 cups (375 mL)
Unsalted butter	1/2 cup (125 mL), approximately, for frying

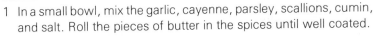

1 In a small bowl, mix the garlic, cayenne, parsley, scallions, cumin, and salt. Roll the pieces of butter in the spices until well coated.

2 Flatten each chicken breast to a thickness of 1/4 inch (5 mm) and cut each half in two. Place a wedge of seasoned butter in the centre. Roll each breast around the butter and tuck in the ends. Dust the rolled breast with flour, dip in the beaten egg, then in the coconut. You may secure the roll with thin cotton string.

3 Heat butter in a skillet until it foams. Fry the chicken rolls until golden, turning carefully. Transfer to a casserole and bake at 275°F (140°C) for 10-15 minutes.

Serves 4

EBONY DUCK

Its name was inspired by the rich, warm colour of the skin after the duck has been roasted with soy sauce, honey and red peppers. It is as delicious as it looks and simple to prepare.

Duckling	1 5-lb (2.5-kg)
Fresh ginger root	2-inch (5-cm) piece, peeled and thinly sliced
Soy sauce	1/2 cup (125 mL)
Liquid honey	1/4 cup (50 mL)
Dry sherry or chili-wine	1/2 cup (125mL)
Garlic	4 cloves, peeled and quartered
Crushed red pepper flakes	4 tsp (20 mL)

1 Wash duckling and dry thoroughly inside and out with paper towels. Remove excess fat from body cavity.

2 Rub duck with sliced ginger and place slices of ginger in cavities, then rub with 4 tsp (20 mL) soy sauce and place on a rack in a shallow roasting pan. Let stand for 30 minutes.

3 Bake, uncovered, at 325°F (160°C).

4 Meanwhile combine the remaining soy sauce, honey, sherry, garlic, and red pepper flakes in a saucepan. Bring to a boil, reduce heat, and simmer for 8 minutes, stirring occasionally.

5 After the duck has roasted for 1 1/2 hours, baste with soy sauce mixture. Baste again after another half hour and continue roasting for 1/2 hour. Duck will roast for a total of 2 1/2 hours.

Serves 2-4

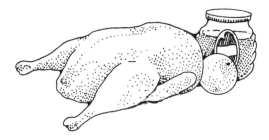

DUCK CURRY

Large pieces of duck in a spiced, coconut-based sauce. Make it a meal with rice and one or two curried vegetables.

Duckling	5 lbs (2 kg), approximately
Dessicated coconut	2 1/2 cups (625 mL)
Boiling water	2 1/2 cups (625 mL)
Butter	2 Tbsp (25 mL)
Onions	2, finely chopped
Garlic	4 cloves, crushed
Fresh ginger root	2-inch (5-cm) piece, peeled and chopped
Turmeric	1 1/2 tsp (7 mL)
Ground coriander	1 1/2 tsp (7 mL)
Ground cumin	1 tsp (5 mL)
Ground fenugreek	1/2 tsp (2 mL)
Cayenne	1 Tbsp (15 mL)
Fresh hot green chilies	4, split lengthways
Fresh lemon juice	2 Tbsp (25 mL)
Salt	1/2 tsp (2 mL) or to taste

1 In a blender, combine coconut and boiling water and process for 1 minute. Pour into a cheesecloth-lined strainer and press with a spoon to extract milk.

2 Melt butter in a Dutch oven. Add onions, garlic, and ginger and sauté until onions are golden. Add the turmeric, coriander, cumin, fenugreek, and cayenne. Sauté for five minutes.

3 Remove the skin from the duck and cut duck into serving pieces. Add the pieces to the Dutch oven and fry in the spices for 10 minutes, stirring constantly. Pour in the coconut milk. Add the hot green chilies and bring to a boil. Cover pan. Reduce heat and simmer for 1-1 1/2 hours, or until duck is tender.

4 Remove duck to a platter and boil sauce until reduced to about 1 cup (250 mL). Skim off fat. Stir in lemon juice and season with salt. Return duck to pan to reheat; turn pieces to coat with sauce.

Serves 4

DUCK WITH PECANS

Many specialty butcher shops sell pieces of duck. If you cannot buy duck breasts, cut up a whole duck and use a combination of legs, thighs, and breast. Serve this with steamed rice and stir-fried snow peas.

Vegetable oil	4 Tbsp (60 mL)
Pecan halves	1/2 cup (125 mL)
Duck breasts	4, skinned, boned and halved
Onion	1 medium, coarsely chopped
Garlic	3 cloves, minced
Mushrooms	1 cup (250 mL), sliced
Green bell pepper	1, seeded and chopped
Crushed dried red chilies	2 tsp (10 mL)
Salt	1/2 tsp (2 mL) or to taste
Brown sugar	2 Tbsp (25 mL)
Chicken broth	1 cup (250 mL)
Cornstarch	1 Tbsp (15 mL)

1 Heat the oil in a deep, heavy skillet. Brown the pecans very briefly. Remove and drain the pecans.

2 Add the duck breast halves to the pan and cook for about 3 minutes, or just until the meat is barely cooked. Add the onion, garlic, mushrooms, green pepper, and crushed chilies and stir with the duck. Cook 3 to 5 minutes, stirring frequently.

3 Mix the salt and brown sugar into the chicken broth and add to the pan. Bring to a boil slowly.

4 Dissolve the cornstarch in 1 Tbsp (15 mL) of cold water. Add the mixture to the pan and stir until the liquid is thickened and clear.

5 Return the pecans to the pan. Toss well. Serve immediately.

Serves 4

MEATS

BEEF CUBES WITH CAYENNE AND SPINACH

Based on an African dish called *kontumbre*, this is a colourful main meal of cubes of beef coated with cayenne and fried with onions, spinach, and tomato sauce. It's wonderful. Swiss chard may be substituted for the spinach.

Top sirloin beef	1 1/4 lb (560 g)
Fresh lemon juice	4 Tbsp (60 mL)
Cayenne	4 1/2 tsp (22 mL)
Ground cumin	1 tsp (5 mL)
Vegetable oil	2 Tbsp (25 mL)
Onion	1, chopped
Spinach	10 oz (280 g), about 8 cups packed
Beef broth	1/2 cup (125 mL)
Tomato sauce	1/2 cup (125 mL)
Salt	1 tsp (5 mL) or to taste
Freshly ground pepper	1/2 tsp (2 mL) or to taste

1 Trim meat and cut into 1-inch (2.5-cm) cubes. Place meat in a bowl and sprinkle with lemon juice. Marinate for 2 hours. Remove from marinade and toss in a paper bag with cayenne and cumin.

2 Heat oil in a skillet and sauté half of the meat at a time, until lightly browned. Remove meat to a platter. Sauté onion until soft.

3 Cook spinach and drain well. Add spinach, beef broth, tomato sauce, salt, and pepper to onions. Mix well, then add the meat and the juices that have accumulated. Heat thoroughly and serve on a bed of rice.

Serves 4

SPICED BEEF SALAD WITH FRESH CORIANDER

The appeal of this Thai salad from the Bangkok Garden Restaurant in Toronto is the contrast between the cool crunch of the raw vegetables and the barely-cooked meatiness of the beef. On the menu it's called "The Royal Barge" and served in hollowed-out cucumber boats.

Flank steak	1 lb (450 g)
Fresh coriander	1 bunch (6-10 stalks)
Fresh mint	10 stalks
Shallots	3, peeled and sliced
Hot red or green chilies	4, sliced
Scallions	2, sliced
Carrot	1, thinly sliced
Cucumber	1, peeled and sliced
Tomatoes	2, cut in wedges
Leaf lettuce	1 small head, coarsely torn
Fresh lime juice	3-5 Tbsp (50-75 mL)
Fish sauce (Nam pla)	2-4 Tbsp (25-60 mL)
	(from Oriental specialty stores)

1 Broil meat medium rare. Allow to cool slightly, then slice thinly across the grain.

2 Remove leaves from coriander and mint. Discard the stalks and leave the leaves whole.

3 Combine all ingredients and toss to mix thoroughly. Adjust seasoning by adding more fish sauce or lime juice.

4 Serve immediately as the fish sauce and lime juice will cause the vegetables to wilt quickly.

Serves 4

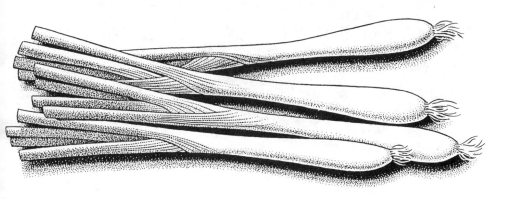

GINGERED CHINESE BEEF

This recipe employs chunkier pieces of beef and longer cooking than you may expect in a Chinese recipe, but the slow blending with the flavours of the ginger and sherry makes them tender and pungent. The plum sauce is available at Oriental specialty stores.

Boneless, lean beef	2 lbs (900 g)
Soy sauce	3 Tbsp (50 mL)
Dry sherry	3 Tbsp (50 mL)
Plum sauce	3 Tbsp (50 mL)
Red wine vinegar	1 Tbsp (15 mL)
Sugar	1 tsp (5 mL)
Peanut oil	3 Tbsp (50 mL)
Garlic	4 cloves, chopped
Ginger	2 Tbsp (25 mL)
Crushed dried red chilies	1 tsp (5 mL)

1 Dry beef cubes thoroughly with paper towels. In a small bowl combine soy sauce, sherry, plum sauce, vinegar, and sugar. Mix well.

2 In a heavy saucepan with a lid or Dutch oven heat peanut oil over high heat. Add garlic, ginger, and chilies and fry for a few seconds. Add beef and brown on all sides.

3 Stir in soy sauce-sherry mixture and cover. Cook over low heat, stirring occasionally, for 2 hours, or until the beef is very tender. Serve with steamed rice.

Serves 4

BEEF KUNG PAO

A wok dish of thinly sliced beef spiced with lots of garlic and ginger, intensified by twenty dried chilies. Serve with steamed rice.

Flank steak	1, about 2 lbs (900 g)
Vegetable oil	2 Tbsp (25 mL)
Scallions	2, chopped
Garlic	5 cloves
Fresh ginger root	4 slices, peeled
Dried red chilies	20
Dry-roasted peanuts	1/2 cup (125 mL)
Dry sherry	2 Tbsp (25 mL)
Soy sauce	3 Tbsp (50 mL)
Red wine vinegar	2 Tbsp (25 mL)
Sugar	1 tsp (5 mL)
Cornstarch	1 1/2 tsp (7 mL)
Water	1 Tbsp (15 mL)
Sesame oil	2 tsp (10 mL)

1 Slice steak thinly across the grain. Arrange scallions, garlic, ginger, red chilies, and peanuts on a plate. Mix the sherry, soy sauce, vinegar, sugar, cornstarch, water, and sesame oil in a small bowl.

2 In a skillet or wok, heat the oil until hot, throw in the chili peppers, scallions, garlic, and ginger. Stir and cook until peppers turn dark. Add the peanuts and sliced steak and cook until meat is brown. Stir in soy sauce mixture and cook until sauce has thickened. Serve with hot rice.

Serves 4

PEPPERED CHILI

The name should warn you that this is as hot as they come. It uses nearly every kind of chili pepper and chili-pepper-based spice. Serve with cornbread for poultice and a green salad for cooling crunch.

BASIL

Beef shoulder	1 lb (450 g)
Butter	3 Tbsp (50 mL)
Garlic	2 cloves, finely chopped
Onions	3, chopped
Green bell pepper	1, cored, seeded and finely chopped
Lean ground beef	1 lb (450 g)
Vegetable oil	1 Tbsp (15 mL)
Mild chili powder	3 Tbsp (50 mL)
Tomatoes	3 large, peeled and chopped
Sugar	1 tsp (5 mL)
Bay leaf	1
Dried basil	1/2 tsp (2 mL)
Dried thyme	1/2 tsp (2 mL)
Paprika	1/2 tsp (2 mL)
Cayenne	1/2 tsp (2 mL)
Crushed dried red chilies	1 tsp (5 mL)
Soy sauce	1 tsp (5 mL)
Tabasco sauce	1 tsp (5 mL)
Pickled serrano or jalapeño peppers	6, finely chopped
Dry red wine	1/2 cup (125 mL)
Beef broth	3/4 cup (175 mL)
Cooked kidney beans	3 cups (750 mL), drained
Salt	1 tsp (5 mL)
Freshly ground pepper	1 tsp (5 mL)

1 Trim beef and cut into strips 1/2 × 1/2 × 2 inches (1.5 × 1.5 × 5 cm).

2 Melt 2 Tbsp (25 mL) butter in a Dutch oven over medium heat. Add the garlic, onions, and green pepper. Sauté for 5 minutes, then add ground beef. Cook until meat is browned.

3 Meanwhile, melt remaining butter and combine with vegetable oil in a skillet. Sauté the beef strips until brown. Transfer beef strips to the Dutch oven. Stir in remaining ingredients except kidney beans, salt and pepper. Simmer, covered, over low heat for 1-1 1/2 hours until beef strips are tender. Add the drained beans and cook for 1/2 hour longer. Season with salt and freshly ground pepper.

Serves 4-6

TEX-MEX CHILI

This is an Americanized version of the Mexican dish. It's not of the purist bent which usually requires much more beans than meat, or meat, when you have it, in large chunks. The cinnamon and allspice are flattering to the cheese and onion. This is a chili we all can identify with (especially if we enjoy identifying with the chili for a while after dinner). Serve with cold beer to warm friends. Leftovers make good fillings for tacos.

Oil	2 Tbsp (25 mL)
Ground beef	1 1/2 lbs (675 g)
Bay leaves	6
Onion	1 large, chopped
Garlic	4 cloves, finely chopped
Ground cinnamon	1/2 tsp (2 mL)
Allspice	1/2 tsp (2 mL)
Crushed dried red chilies	2 tsp (10 mL)
Salt	1 tsp (5 mL)
Chili powder	2 Tbsp (25 mL)
Ground cumin	1 tsp (5 mL)
Dried oregano	1/2 tsp (2 mL)
Vinegar	1 Tbsp (15 mL)
Tomato paste	1 5 1/2-oz (156-mL) can
Water	5 cups (1.25 L)
Cooked kidney beans	1 1/2 cups (375 mL) drained
Cheddar cheese	1/2 cup (125 mL) grated
Onion	1 small, finely chopped

1 Heat the oil in a Dutch oven over medium-high heat. Add the beef and cook until meat is evenly browned. Add the bay leaves, onion, garlic, cinnamon, allspice, dried chilies, salt, chili powder, cumin, and oregano. Cook, stirring occasionally, for 5 minutes.

2 Stir in vinegar, tomato paste, and water. Simmer, uncovered, for 1 hour. Add the kidney beans and simmer for 1/2 hour longer. Serve in large bowls and top with grated cheese and raw chopped onion.

Serves 4

PICADILLO

Not to be confused with picalilli, the relish, or peccadillo which refers to the more relishing spices of life. This is a mealy, wonderful mixture of spiced meat, raisins, olives, and tomatoes. It may also be used as a filling for meat pie.

Olive oil	3 Tbsp (50 mL)
Lean ground beef	1 1/2 lb (675 g)
Onions	2, chopped
Garlic	2 large cloves
Tomatoes	3, peeled and chopped
Pickled jalapeño peppers	4, sliced
Raisins (Thompson are best)	1/2 cup (125 mL)
Pimento-stuffed olives	1/2 cup (125 mL) sliced
Dried thyme	1/4 tsp (1 mL)
Dried oregano	1/4 tsp (1 mL)
Salt	1 tsp (5 mL)
Freshly ground pepper	1 tsp (5 mL)

1 Heat oil in a large skillet and brown the meat. Add the onions and garlic and cook until onions are soft. Stir in remaining ingredients and simmer, uncovered, for about 20 minutes until raisins have plumped and nearly all the liquid has been absorbed. Serve over hot rice or over polenta.

Serves 4

Ebony Duck (top); Potato and Tomato Curry

STEAK TARTARE

Traditionally steak tartare is a bit spicy, and this recipe is even more spicy than traditional. Note the use of Tabasco, cayenne and fresh black pepper. These condiments don't require cooking to bring out their best flavours, whereas others, like crushed chili peppers, can taste quite raw and painful. Serve the steak tartare on toast points.

Lean boneless sirloin	1 lb (450 g), chopped fine
Worcestershire sauce	2 tsp (10 mL)
Tabasco	2 tsp (10 mL)
Egg yolk	1 large
Olive oil	2 Tbsp (25 mL)
Red wine vinegar	2 Tbsp (25 mL)
Capers	1 Tbsp (15 mL) minced
Anchovy fillet	1 tsp (5 mL) minced
Onion	2 Tbsp (25 mL) minced
Cayenne	1 tsp (5 mL)
Freshly ground pepper	1 tsp (5 mL)
Cognac	2 Tbsp (25 mL)
Fresh parsley	1 tsp (5 mL) minced, for garnish
Onion	1 tsp (5 mL) minced, for garnish

1 In a bowl combine all ingredients except for the garnish and mix thoroughly.

2 Shape the steak tartare lightly into 4 patties.

3 Place on chilled plates and garnish with minced parsley and onions.

Serves 4

GREEN CHILI

This is chili without the beans. Pieces of pork are slow-cooked with a large amount of green chilies until the meat is very moist and tender. Those with more delicate palates should begin carefully — use fewer green chilies than this intense recipe calls for. Serve with crisp tortillas.

Boneless pork shoulder	2 lbs (900 g), cut in 1/2-inch (1.5-cm) cubes
Lard	3 Tbsp (50 mL)
Flour	1/4 cup (50 mL)
Onions	2 medium, chopped
Garlic	3 cloves, finely chopped
Fresh green chilies	1 cup (250 mL), seeded and chopped
Ripe tomatoes	3 cups (750 mL), peeled
Tomato paste	1 5 1/2-oz (156-mL) can
Water	2 cups (500 mL)
Dried oregano	1/2 tsp (2 mL)
Salt	1 tsp (5 mL)
Freshly ground pepper	1 tsp (5 mL)

1 Melt the lard in a heavy skillet over medium-high heat. Coat the pork cubes with flour and add to the skillet, a few at a time. When cubes are browned, transfer to a Dutch oven.

2 Add the onions and garlic to the skillet. Cook until the onions are translucent, then add to the pork cubes. Stir remaining ingredients, except salt and pepper, into Dutch oven. Simmer, uncovered, for 1 hour, stirring often. Season with salt and freshly ground pepper.

Serves 4

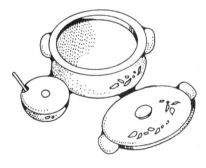

TAMALE PIE

This is a layered casserole constructed on the same principle as lasagne, using cornmeal, spicy meat, and cheese. It is lovely served with a crisp green salad and light beer.

Beef broth	4 cups (1 L)
Cornmeal	1 1/2 cups (375 mL)
Salt	1 tsp (5 mL)
Eggs	2, beaten
Parmesan or Cheddar cheese	3/4 cup (175 mL)
Ground beef	1 lb (450 g)
Vegetable oil	1 Tbsp (15 mL)
Fresh hot chilies	2, seeded and chopped
Onion	1 large, chopped
Green pepper	1, seeded and chopped
Garlic	3 cloves, minced
Dried oregano	1/2 tsp (2 mL)
Ground cumin	1/2 tsp (2 mL)
Cornmeal	1 Tbsp (15 mL)
Water	1/4 cup (50 mL)
Tomatoes	4, peeled and diced
Whole kernel corn	1 1/4 cups (300 mL)
Ripe olives	1/2 cup (125 mL) pitted and sliced
Cheddar cheese	2 cups (500 mL) grated

1 Stir 1 cup (250 mL) broth into cornmeal. Heat remaining broth over direct heat in top of double boiler and add the cornmeal. Cook over low heat, stirring constantly until mixture is thick. Stir in salt.

2 Fill bottom of double boiler with boiling water and place cornmeal over it. Cover and cook for 20 minutes.

3 Stir 1/4 cup (50 mL) hot cornmeal into beaten eggs, then pour into remaining corn meal, along with Parmesan cheese. Mix well and remove from heat.

4 Brown beef in hot oil. Add the chilies, onion, green pepper, garlic, oregano, and cumin. Stir and cook over low heat for 10 minutes.

5 Blend 1 Tbsp (15 mL) cornmeal with water and add, along with the tomatoes and corn, to meat mixture. Cook over medium heat, stirring until mixture boils and thickens. Remove from heat and stir in olives.

6 Grease a 9-inch × 13-inch (3.5-L) casserole and line bottom and sides with half the cornmeal mixture. Fill centre with meat mixture and spoon remaining cornmeal mixture over top. Sprinkle with grated Cheddar cheese.

7 Bake in 350°F (180°C) oven for 25-30 minutes.

Serves 6-8

HOT RED GOULASH

Buy the hottest paprika you can for this goulash, but if you still find the dish too mild, don't add more paprika than is required in the recipe; the goulash will become bitter. Add a few dashes of hot pepper sauce instead.

Lean pork shoulder	1 1/2 lbs (675 g), cubed
Olive oil	2 Tbsp (25 mL)
Garlic	3 cloves, finely minced
Onions	2, chopped
Paprika	3 Tbsp (50 mL)
Flour	2 Tbsp (25 mL)
Marjoram	1/2 tsp (2 mL)
Green pepper	1 large, seeded and cut in thin strips
Peeled plum tomatoes	1 1/2 cups (375 mL)
Chicken stock	1/2 cup (125 mL)
Sauerkraut	1 1/2 lbs (675 g), drained
Salt	1/2 tsp (5 mL) or to taste
Freshly ground pepper	1/2 tsp (5 mL) or to taste
Sour cream	1 cup (250 mL)

1 Heat the olive oil in a Dutch oven and sauté the garlic, onions, and paprika until the onions are limp.

2 Roll the meat in the flour and add the onions, cooking only enough to lightly brown. Sprinkle with the marjoram.

3 Add the green pepper, tomatoes, chicken stock and sauerkraut. Bring to a boil, then reduce heat, cover and simmer for 1 hour, or until the meat is tender. Season with salt and freshly ground pepper.

4 Serve very hot with sour cream spooned over the goulash.

Serves 4

HOT AND SOUR SPARERIBS

Spareribs in a clear sauce with pretty flecks of green scallions, red chilies, and ginger.

Meaty pork spareribs	1 1/2 lbs (675 g), cut into 1-inch (2.5-cm) pieces
Soy sauce	1 Tbsp (15 mL)
Cornstarch	1/2 cup (125 mL)
Water	3 Tbsp (50 mL)
Peanut oil	3 1/4 cups (800 mL)
Fresh hot red chilies	2, shredded
Garlic	1 large clove, finely minced
Fresh ginger root	2 tsp (10 mL) peeled and finely minced
Scallions	3, finely chopped
Sugar	3 Tbsp (50 mL)
Vinegar	3 Tbsp (50 mL)

1 Place ribs in a bowl. Mix together soy sauce, 1 Tbsp (15 mL) corn-starch and water. Pour over ribs and let marinate for 10 minutes, then drain. Toss the ribs in a plastic bag with rest of the cornstarch.

2 Heat all except 2 Tbsp (25 mL) oil in a wok or deep skillet to 350°F (180°C). Shake off excess cornstarch and drop a few ribs at a time in the hot oil. Fry for 6 minutes, stirring to keep ribs from sticking. Turn off heat and scoop out ribs. Drain and let cool for 2-5 minutes. Reheat oil and fry ribs again until crisp and brown. Remove from oil and drain on paper towels.

3 To make sauce, heat 2 Tbsp (25 mL) oil in another wok or skillet. Add the hot chilies, garlic, ginger, and scallions and stir-fry for 2 minutes. Stir in the ribs.

4 Dissolve the sugar in vinegar and add to skillet. Toss to coat the ribs evenly.

Serves 2 as a main dish or 4 as an appetizer

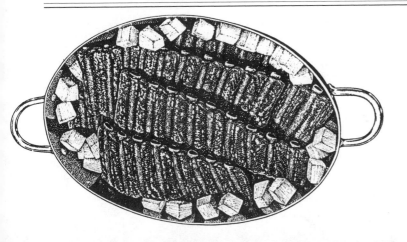

RED HOT SPARERIBS

Serve these with cornbread, or if you think you can take more heat, try the recipe for garlic-chili toast.

Garlic	6 cloves, crushed and finely chopped
Onions	2, chopped
Tomato sauce	2 1/4 cups (550 mL)
Red wine vinegar	1/3 cup (75 mL)
Worcestershire sauce	1/3 cup (75 mL)
Bay leaves	2
Dried oregano	1/4 tsp (1 mL)
Cayenne	2 tsp (5 mL)
Brown sugar	1/2 cup (125 mL)
Meaty spareribs	4 lbs (1.8 kg), cut into 4 servings

1 Put garlic, onions, tomato sauce, bay leaves, vinegar, and Worcestershire sauce in a saucepan. Bring to a boil, then reduce heat and simmer, uncovered, for 30 minutes. Stir in the oregano, cayenne, and brown sugar.

2 While sauce is simmering, cover ribs with foil, but do not seal, and bake at 450°F (230°C) for 15 minutes. Reduce heat to 350°F (180°C) and pour sauce over the meat. Cover again loosely with foil and bake for 45 minutes, basting several times. Uncover and bake 30-40 minutes longer, basting several times until richly glazed.

Serves 4

PORK CHOPS WITH SPICY ORANGE SAUCE

The meat is browned, then napped with a spicy-sweet sauce of orange, honey, ginger, and fresh hot red chilies. Pork chops were never like this. Serve them with steamed rice and a green vegetable.

Pork chops	4, about 1 1/4 lbs (550 g)
Flour	2 Tbsp (25 mL)
Vegetable oil	2 Tbsp (25 mL)
Onion	1, chopped
Green pepper	1, seeded and cut in strips
Fresh hot red chili	1, seeded and minced
Fresh orange juice	1 cup (250 mL)
Grated orange rind	grated rind of 1/2 orange
Soy sauce	1 Tbsp (15 mL)
Ground ginger	1 tsp (5 mL)
Chicken broth	1/2 cup (125 mL)
Honey	2 Tbsp (30 mL)
Oranges	2, peeled and sectioned

1 Trim excess fat from meat and lightly dust with flour. Heat oil in a skillet, brown pork chops on both sides, then remove from skillet. To skillet add onion, green pepper, and chili. Sauté for 3 minutes.

2 Return chops to skillet and add orange juice, grated rind, soy sauce, ginger, chicken broth, and honey. Stir to combine well. Bring to the boil, then reduce heat and simmer for 20 minutes. Turn chops several times.

3 Just before serving, add orange segments.

Serves 2-4

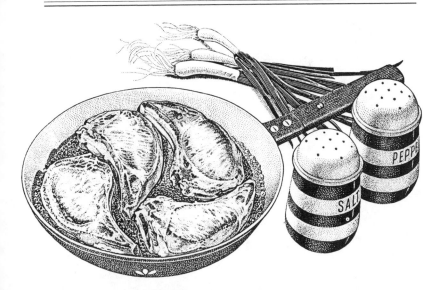

MIDDLE EASTERN SAUSAGES

These are skinless, spicy sausages that should be served slightly rare with rice and sautéed eggplant. They are also good in a pita bread sandwich with salad.

Ground lamb	1 1/2 lbs (675 g)
Garlic	3 cloves, finely minced
Egg	1, lightly beaten
Pine nuts	1/4 cup (50 mL)
Fresh parsley	1/4 cup (50 mL) finely minced
Salt	1/2 tsp (2 mL)
Freshly ground pepper	1/2 tsp (2 mL)
Cayenne	1 Tbsp (15 mL)
Olive oil	1/2 cup (125 mL), for frying

1 Mix the lamb, garlic, egg, pine nuts, parsley, salt, pepper, and cayenne. Form mixture into tiny sausage shapes.

2 Heat olive oil in a large skillet and sauté the sausages. Shake the skillet continuously while the sausages are browning. Cook over medium heat about 3 minutes. Take care not to overcook; they should be slightly rare in the centre.

Serves 4

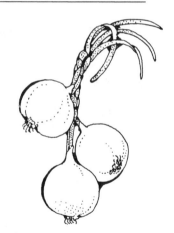

SPICED LAMB CHOPS WITH CASHEWS AND POPPY SEEDS

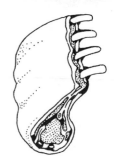

The ingredients themselves tell the story of these tender chops, flavoured with yoghurt and decorated with cashews and poppy seeds. But they're not just another pretty face — there's personality from the power of cayenne, cloves, ginger, and cardamon. A glass of rich red wine is terrific with these.

Rib lamb chops	8, 3/4-inch (2-cm) thick
Butter	1/4 cup (50 mL)
Onions	1 cup (250 mL) finely chopped
Garlic	2 Tbsp (25 mL) finely chopped
Fresh ginger root	1 Tbsp (25 mL) peeled and minced
Raw cashew nuts	1/2 cup (125 mL)
Poppy seeds	2 tsp (10 mL)
Whole cloves	4
Cardamon seeds	1/2 tsp (1 mL)
Bay leaves	2
Cayenne	2 Tbsp (25 mL)
Yoghurt	1 cup (250 mL)
Ground cardamon	1 tsp (5 mL)
Freshly ground pepper	2 tsp (10 mL)
Ground cinnamon	1/4 tsp (1 mL)
Ground cloves	1/4 tsp (1 mL)
Salt	1/2 tsp (2 mL) or to taste
Fresh parsley	2 Tbsp (25 mL) chopped

1 Trim the fat from the lamb chops. Set aside.

2 Heat butter in a large heavy frying pan. Add the onions, garlic, ginger, cashews, poppy seeds, whole cloves, cardamon seeds, bay leaves, and cayenne. Sauté until onions are translucent.

3 Push onion and spice mixture to the side of the pan. Add the lamb chops and lightly brown in the pan.

4 When chops are browned, add yoghurt, cardamon, black pepper, cinnamon, and cloves. Mix well. Cover and simmer for 1/2 hour, or until meat is tender.

5 Remove cover and increase heat to reduce sauce. Add salt to taste and garnish with chopped parsley. Serve with hot rice.

Serves 4

SPICED LEG OF LAMB WITH FRESH GINGER AND GARLIC

Twenty-five cloves of garlic and a large piece of fresh ginger are puréed with cayenne to make a paste that infuses the meat with spice and succulence. You can serve the finished lamb Western-style, with a starch and green vegetable, and full-bodied red wine, or use it to highlight a spicy, multi-course ecumenical dinner.

Boned leg of lamb	4 1/2-5 lbs (2-2.5 kg)
Fresh ginger root	4-inch (10-cm) piece, peeled and thinly sliced
Garlic	25 medium cloves
Cayenne	2 Tbsp (25 mL)
Red wine vinegar	1/4 cup (50 mL)
Salt	1 tsp (5 mL)
Butter	2 Tbsp (25 mL)

1 In a blender or food processor, process the ginger, garlic, 1 Tbsp (12.5 mL) cayenne, and red wine vinegar until it forms a paste.

2 Stuff the cavity of the leg of lamb with the spice paste. Score the surface and rub the salt and 1 Tbsp (12.5 mL) cayenne evenly over the surface. Dot with butter.

3 Bake at 350°F (180°C) for 1 1/2 hours-2 hours, depending how well done you like your lamb. Baste several times with pan juices during baking. Remove to a platter and let rest for 15 minutes before carving.

Serves 6

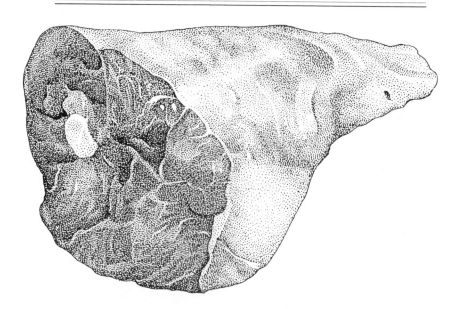

LEFTOVER LAMB CURRY

Should there be any lamb left over from the spiced leg of lamb which precedes this recipe, it can be turned into an exceptional and fast curry. Cubes of cooked lamb are coated with fresh lemon juice and braised in a curry mixture. Look for Madras curry mixture at East Indian specialty stores. Serve the dish with steamed rice, toasted almonds, and yoghurt.

Butter	5 Tbsp (75 mL)
Onions	2 cups (500 mL) thinly sliced
Garlic	4 tsp (20 mL) finely chopped
Cold roast leg of lamb	2 cups (500 mL) cut into 2-inch (5-cm) pieces, trimmed of all fat and gristle
Lemon juice	4 Tbsp (60 mL)
Salt	1 tsp (5 mL)
Imported Madras curry powder	3 Tbsp (50 mL)
Flour	1 Tbsp (15 mL)
Vegetable oil	1 Tbsp (15 mL)
Beef stock	1 cup (250 mL)

1 Preheat the oven to 325°F (160°C).

2 Melt 2 Tbsp butter (25 mL) in a 2 or 3 quart (2-3 L) heavy flame-proof casserole with a tight-fitting cover. Add the onions and garlic and fry over moderate heat for about 10 minutes, stirring every now and then, until they are soft and lightly coloured. Transfer them from the casserole to a small bowl.

3 Dip the pieces of meat in the lemon juice, sprinkle with a little salt, then roll them in the curry powder combined with flour, coating them heavily. Heat the remaining 3 Tbsp (50 mL) of butter and the tablespoon of vegetable oil in the casserole. When the foam subsides, fry the lamb over moderately high heat, a few pieces at a time, until each piece is a deep golden brown. Return the onions to the casserole, pour in the stock, and bring to a boil, stirring gently to combine all the ingredients. Then cover the casserole tightly, and bake for 1 hour.

Serves 2-4

LAMB CURRY

A treasured recipe from Surrender Massih, its spice heat is balanced by a fragrance of cloves, paprika, and fresh ginger. Serve with hot rice and a raita made from chopped fresh tomatoes and yoghurt.

Boneless lean lamb	2 lbs (900 g), cubed
Vegetable oil	3 Tbsp (50 mL)
Cloves	6 whole
Onions	3, diced
Garlic	5 cloves, halved
Fresh ginger root	1-inch (2.5-cm) piece, peeled and finely diced
Paprika	1/4 tsp (1 mL)
Curry powder	1/2 tsp (2 mL)
Dried crushed red chilies	1 tsp (5 mL)
Turmeric	1/4 tsp (1 mL)
Salt	2 tsp (2 mL)
Fresh hot green chilies	2, finely diced
Green bell peppers	2, cored and cut in strips
Ripe tomatoes	3 large, coarsely diced
Fresh lemon juice	2 Tbsp (25 mL)

1 Heat vegetable oil in a Dutch oven. Toss in the whole cloves and fry for 30 seconds, then add onions and garlic. Cook, stirring often, until onions begin to brown. Add cubed lamb and continue cooking until lamb is nicely browned. Scrape the bottom of the pot often while lamb is cooking.

2 In a small bowl, mix together the fresh ginger, paprika, curry powder, crushed red chilies, turmeric, and salt. Sprinkle half the combined spices over the lamb. Add the diced green chilies and green pepper strips and continue cooking for 5 minutes, stirring constantly.

3 Add the lemon juice, remainder of the spices, and diced tomatoes. Cover and simmer for 20-30 minutes. Add a small amount of water, if necessary.

Serves 4-6

RABBIT IN MUSTARD

Pieces of rabbit are swabbed in hot mustard, roasted in wine, then served in a cream sauce made with pan juices. The mustard mellows in the roasting. Serve this simple recipe with garlic potatoes and a green vegetable.

THYME

Hot prepared mustard	3 Tbsp (50 mL)
Fresh bread crumbs	2 Tbsp (25 mL)
Olive oil	4 1/2 tsp (22 mL)
Rabbit	3 lbs (1.4 kg)
Dry white wine	1 cup (250 mL)
Light cream	1 cup (250 mL)
Salt	1/2 tsp (2 mL)
Freshly ground pepper	1/2 tsp (2 mL)
Dried thyme	1/2 tsp (2 mL)

1 Mix together mustard, bread crumbs, and olive oil. Cut rabbit into serving-size pieces.

2 Completely coat pieces of meat with mustard mixture. Place in a roasting pan and pour the wine over the meat. Roast at 400°F (200°C) until meat is tender; this will take about 45 minutes.

3 Remove meat to a warm serving platter. Place roasting pan over high heat and add the cream, salt, pepper, and thyme. Bring to a boil and boil for 3-4 minutes.

4 Pour some of the sauce over the meat and serve the rest in a gravy boat.

Serves 4

VEGETABLES AND SALADS

SZECHUAN-STYLE GREEN BEANS

Little specks of spice and meat cling to the crisp beans to create an effect of crunch and spice.

Green beans	1 1/2 lb (675 g)
Peanut oil	1 cup (250 mL)
Ground pork	1/4 lb (110 g)
Tung choy (Chinese preserved winter vegetables	1 Tbsp (15 mL) minced
Garlic	1 large clove, finely minced
Fresh ginger root	1/4-inch (5-mm) piece, peeled and minced
Chili sauce (available in specialty stores)	1 tsp (5 mL)
Soy sauce	2 Tbsp (25 mL)
Dry sherry	2 Tbsp (25 mL)
Sugar	1/2 tsp (2 mL)
Water	2 Tbsp (25 mL)
Vinegar	1 tsp (5 mL)
Sesame oil	1 Tbsp (15 mL)
Scallions	2, finely minced

1 Snip off ends of green beans, rinse and dry thoroughly. Arrange pork, tung choy, garlic, and ginger on a small plate. Mix together seasonings.

2 Heat peanut oil in a wok or large skillet until almost smoking (375°F or 190°C). Deep fry beans until they are wrinkled and slightly blistered, stirring constantly. Pour beans and oil into a strainer over a bowl.

3 Re-heat 3 Tbsp (50 mL) of the oil in the wok or skillet. Add the pork and fry until thoroughly cooked, breaking up the lumps so meat is in tiny pieces. Add the tung choy, garlic, ginger, and chili sauce. Stir-fry for 2 minutes. Add the beans, soy sauce, sherry, sugar, water, vinegar, sesame oil, and scallions. Stir vigorously until the liquid is absorbed.

Serves 4

CURRIED CAULIFLOWER WITH LIME

A colourful dish that's tart, hot, and wonderful. Don't reduce the amount of salt. Fenugreek, which has a flavour a bit like celery seeds, is often used in curried dishes. It can be found in many supermarkets or in Oriental specialty stores.

Cauliflower	1 medium head
Butter	1/4 cup (50 mL)
Onion	1 medium, chopped
Garlic	3 cloves, finely minced
Ground cumin	1 tsp (5 mL)
Turmeric	1 tsp (5 mL)
Ground coriander	1/2 tsp (2 mL)
Salt	1 tsp (5 mL)
Freshly ground pepper	pinch
Fenugreek seeds	1/2 tsp (2 mL)
Crushed dried red chilies	2 tsp (10 mL)
Fresh lime juice	2 Tbsp (25 mL)
Water	1/4 cup (50 mL)
Fresh or frozen peas	1/2 cup (125 mL)

1 Separate cauliflower into flowerets of uniform size. Heat butter in a large saucepan, and sauté onion, garlic, cumin, turmeric, coriander, salt, pepper, fenugreek seeds, and red chilies for 5 minutes until onion is translucent. Add lime juice and water. Stir in flowerets. Cover, and cook over low heat for 15 minutes, stirring twice during this time. Stir in peas and cook for 2 more minutes.

Serves 4

CAULIFLOWER-EGGPLANT BHAJI

This is a well-spiced, hot dish that includes potatoes, peas, and tomatoes in support of the cauliflower and eggplant. Bhaji is a drier dish than curry, although it is flavoured with many of the same spices.

Cauliflower	1 small
Eggplant	1 small
Oil	2 Tbsp (25 mL)
Black mustard seeds	1 tsp (5 mL)
Turmeric	1 tsp (5 mL)
Ground cumin	1 tsp (5 mL)
Cayenne	1 tsp (5 mL)
Ground ginger	1/2 tsp (2 mL)
Ground coriander	1/2 tsp (2 mL)
Ground cinnamon	1/4 tsp (1 mL)
Salt	1/2 tsp (2 mL)
Water	1/4 cup (50 mL)
Fresh hot green chilies	2, minced
Potato	1, diced and parboiled
Fresh or frozen peas	1 cup (250 mL)
Tomato	1, diced
Fresh lemon juice	1-2 Tbsp (15-25 mL)

1 Separate cauliflower into small flowerets and stems and dice. Cut eggplant into 1/2-inch (1-cm) cubes.

2 Heat oil in a large saucepan. When hot, add the mustard seeds, turmeric, cumin, cayenne, ginger, coriander, cinnamon and salt. Fry for 30 seconds.

3 Add the cauliflower and stir in 1/4 cup (50 mL) water. Add the eggplant, chilies and potatoes. Cook over low heat for 10 minutes, gently stirring from time to time, then add peas. Continue cooking for another 5 minutes. It may be necessary to add a Tbsp (15 mL) of water occasionally.

4 Add the diced tomatoes and lemon juice just before serving.

Serves 4

SPICY EGGPLANT AND TOFU IN BLACK BEAN SAUCE

Try this on someone who claims to dislike eggplant. The combination of spices and textures give the vegetable new meaning.

Eggplant	2 cups (500 mL), peeled and cut into 1/2-inch (1-cm) cubes
Tofu (bean curd)	1 lb (450 g), drained and cut into 1/2-inch (1-cm) cubes
Salt	1/2 tsp (2 mL)
Vegetable oil	4 Tbsp (60 mL)
Scallions	2, minced
Garlic	5 cloves, peeled and minced
Cayenne	1 Tbsp (15 mL)
Salted black beans	3 Tbsp (50 mL)
Soy sauce	2 Tbsp (25 mL)
Vegetable or chicken broth	1 cup (250 mL)
Cornstarch	4 tsp (20 mL)
Water	4 tsp (20 mL)
Szechuan peppercorn powder	1/2 tsp (2 mL)

1 Put eggplant in a strainer, sprinkle with salt and let drain for 15 minutes. Dry on paper towels. Heat the vegetable oil in a skillet or wok. Stir-fry the eggplant cubes over high heat until soft. Remove from pan and set aside.

2 In same pan, stir-fry the scallions, garlic, and cayenne for 1 minute. Add more oil if necessary. Add the salted black beans, soy sauce, and stock and mix well. Add the tofu and eggplant cubes. Cover pan, reduce heat and simmer for 15 minutes, stirring occasionally.

3 Dissolve cornstarch in water and pour into the eggplant-tofu mixture. Cook gently until sauce thickens. Pour into serving dish and sprinkle with peppercorn powder.

Serves 4

GINGER GARLIC TOFU

Note the toasted sesame seeds — in the dark oil and for sprinkling. They lend this dish a smoky-nut flavour which goes well with the ginger. (Don't substitute the light-coloured, cold-pressed sesame oil for the dark. It isn't the same thing at all.)

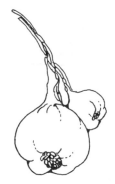

Tofu (bean curd)	1 lb (450 g)
Safflower oil	1/4 cup (50 mL)
Dark sesame oil	2 Tbsp (25 mL)
Onions	2 1/2 cups (625 mL) chopped
Garlic	4 large cloves, pressed
Fresh ginger root	3 Tbsp (50 mL) grated
Vegetable stock or water	1 1/2 cups (375 mL)
Cornstarch	5 tsp (25 mL)
Soy sauce	1/3 cup (75 mL)
Wine vinegar	2 Tbsp (25 mL)
Honey	1 Tbsp (15 mL)
Szechuan chili sauce	2 tsp (10 mL)
Scallions	3, chopped
Toasted sesame seeds	2 Tbsp (25 mL)

1 Cut tofu into 8 slices. Blot on paper towels.

2 Heat safflower and sesame oil in a saucepan and sauté onions, garlic, and ginger for 5 minutes, stirring occasionally. Dissolve cornstarch in the water and add to the onions, along with soy sauce, vinegar, honey, and Szechuan chili sauce. Simmer for 5 minutes.

3 Pour a thin layer of sauce in the bottom of a small casserole. Arrange half of the tofu slices in the dish. Continue layering sauce and tofu, ending with sauce. Bake at 350°F (180°C) for 20-25 minutes.

4 Garnish with scallions and toasted sesame seeds.

Serves 4

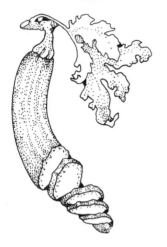

HOT AND SOUR ZUCCHINI

The quick stir-frying of the vegetables preserves the colour and texture and leaves a richly spiced sauce to flavour the rice that should accompany this dish.

Zucchini	1/2 lb (225 g)
Dried red chili peppers	4
Cornstarch	1 tsp (5 mL)
Red or white vinegar	1 Tbsp (15 mL)
Soy sauce	1 tsp (5 mL)
Sugar	2 tsp (10 mL)
Sesame oil	4 Tbsp (60 mL) (from Oriental specialty stores)
Szechuan peppercorns	1 tsp (5 mL)
Fresh ginger root	2 tsp (10 mL) peeled and finely chopped
Garlic	2 tsp (10 mL) finely chopped
Green onions	4, chopped

1 Wash the zucchini and slice into 1/4-inch (5-mm) rounds. Sprinkle lightly with salt and let stand for 10 minutes. Wash and pat dry with paper towels.

2 Cut the stems off the red peppers and shake out the seeds. Slice the peppers lengthwise into thin strips.

3 Mix the cornstarch with the vinegar and soy sauce, then add sugar. Set aside.

4 Heat the sesame oil in a wok. When hot, add the Szechuan peppercorns and red pepper strips. Stir-fry briefly.

5 Add the zucchini, ginger, garlic, and green onions. Toss for about 30 seconds, then add the cornstarch mixture. Mix well and continue to stir-fry for a few seconds until the sauce clings to the zucchini.

Serves 4

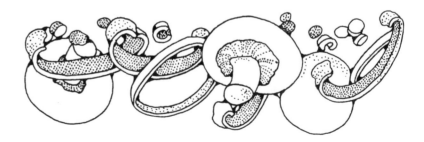

MUSHROOMS WITH JALAPEÑO PEPPERS

This works best with tiny mushrooms, so that each forkful is an exhilarating bite of mushrooms and chilies.

Vegetable oil	3 Tbsp (50 mL)
Butter	3 Tbsp (50 mL)
Button mushrooms	1 lb (450 g), wiped clean
Garlic	2 cloves, finely minced
Pickled jalapeño peppers	4, seeded and sliced
Salt	1/4 tsp (1 mL)
Freshly ground pepper	1/4 tsp (1 mL)

1 Heat the oil and butter in a heavy skillet. When foaming, add the mushrooms, garlic, and chilies. Cook over medium heat, stirring constantly, until mushrooms are lightly browned, about 8 minutes. Season with salt and freshly-ground pepper.

Serves 4

MUSHROOM AND LEEK STIR-FRY WITH TOFU

The oyster mushrooms called for in this recipe have become increasingly popular and can be found in many supermarket produce sections. If not, try Oriental grocery stores. The mushrooms are large, flat, and oyster-coloured.

Leeks	2 cups (500 mL), white part only, cut lengthwise
Vegetable oil	7 tsp (35 mL)
Sliced oyster mushrooms	4 cups (1 L)
Soy sauce	1 Tbsp (15 mL)
Szechuan chili sauce	2 tsp (10 mL)
Tofu (bean curd)	8 oz (225 g), thinly sliced

1 Put the leeks and half the oil in a wok and cook over moderate heat for 2 minutes. Add the mushrooms, soy sauce, and Szechuan chili sauce. Stir-fry until they are cooked, about 2 minutes. Remove from heat.

2 Blot tofu slices on paper towels. In a skillet, heat remaining oil and fry tofu until crisp and golden brown on both sides.

3 Reheat leeks and mushrooms briefly. Turn into a serving dish and arrange tofu on top.

Serves 4

BROILED PEPPERS IN OIL

Broiling the peppers over open heat lends them a smoky, mellow flavour. In the summer, roast the peppers over charcoal and serve them as a side dish with steak or chicken.

Sweet red peppers	3 large
Green or black olives (Italian or Greek)	3/4 cup (175 mL), pitted
Garlic	2 cloves, finely minced
Lemon juice	2 Tbsp (25 mL)
Cayenne	1/2 tsp (2 mL)
Olive oil	2 Tbsp (25 mL)
Salt	1/2 tsp (2 mL) or to taste

1 Broil the whole peppers for 4-8 minutes, 2 inches (5 cm) from heat. To broil them evenly, spear core with a long fork and turn the peppers as their skins blister. Cool until lukewarm. Peel away the skins and remove stem and core. Reserve any juices.

2 Cut peppers into strips and combine with reserved pepper juices, olives, garlic, lemon juice, cayenne, and olive oil. Add salt to taste. Serve the salad immediately or marinate peppers at room temperature for several hours before serving.

Serves 4

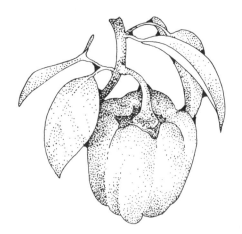

STIR-FRIED PEPPERS WITH ZUCCHINI AND WATER CHESTNUTS

Hot peppers and their cooler cousins are united with other vegetables in a soothing sauce flavoured with oyster sauce and sherry.

Straw mushrooms	1/2 cup (125 mL)
Bamboo shoots	1/2 cup (125 mL) sliced in strips
Zucchini or summer squash	2 1/2 cups (625 mL) sliced in 1-inch (2.5-cm) pieces
Water chestnuts	10
Sweet red pepper	1, seeded
Fresh hot chilies	4
Shallots	10
Water chestnut powder	1 Tbsp (15 mL)
Dry sherry	1 Tbsp (15 mL)
Chicken stock	1/2 cup (125 mL)
Oyster sauce	5 tsp (25 mL)
Soy sauce	1 Tbsp (15 mL)
Sugar	1 Tbsp (15 mL)
Peanut oil	2 Tbsp (25 mL)
Salt	1/2 tsp (2 mL)
Freshly ground pepper	1/2 tsp (2 mL)

1 Rinse mushrooms. Slice water chestnuts. Triangle-cut sweet pepper and hot chilies. Peel and slice shallots. Arrange vegetables on a small platter.

2 Mix together water chestnut powder, sherry, chicken stock, oyster sauce, soy sauce, and sugar and set aside. Heat wok over medium-high heat. Add peanut oil and heat until hot but not smoking. Toss in vegetables and stir-fry for about 4 minutes, or until vegetables are crisp and tender. Stir sauce and add to vegetables. Continue stirring until sauce has thickened. Serve immediately.

Serves 4

LIZ RAINE'S GARLIC POTATOES

Potatoes are a good vehicle for the double bite of minced garlic and chili peppers. This dish works well as part of a buffet because it stays hot for some time.

Potatoes	4 large or 6 medium
Cheddar cheese	4 cups (1 L) grated
Garlic	8 cloves, finely minced
Fresh hot chilies	6, finely chopped
Light cream	3/4 cup (175 mL)

1 Peel potatoes and boil in salted water until tender. Drain, let cool slightly, and slice. Put into a buttered 8 × 8-inch (2-L) baking dish. Sprinkle 2 cups (500 mL) of the cheese, the chilies, and garlic over the potatoes. Sprinkle with remaining cheese and pour cream over top.

2 Bake at 375°F (190°C) for 45 minutes to 1 hour, until cheese is crusty brown and potatoes have absorbed most of the cream.

Serves 4-6

POTATO AND TOMATO CURRY

This makes a terrific main dish at a vegetarian dinner. Fresh coriander can be found in Chinese grocery stores.

Potatoes	6 small
Butter	2 Tbsp (25 mL)
Vegetable oil	2 Tbsp (25 mL)
Turmeric	1 tsp (5 mL)
Ground cumin	1 tsp (5 mL)
Cayenne	2 tsp (10 mL)
Ground cardamon	1/4 tsp (1 mL)
Ground coriander	1 tsp (5 mL)
Fresh ginger root	3-inch (7.5-cm) piece, peeled and minced
Onions	2 medium, peeled and minced
Garlic	4 cloves, peeled and minced
Fresh green chilies	4, sliced
Tomatoes	4 medium, peeled and coarsely chopped
Fresh coriander leaves or parsley	2 Tbsp (25 mL) chopped

1 Boil the potatoes in their skins for 10 minutes. Drain and allow to cook slightly. Peel and slice in 1/2-inch (1-cm) slices.

2 Heat butter and oil in a heavy frying pan and fry the potato slices until golden brown on both sides. Remove from pan.

3 Fry the turmeric, cumin, cayenne, cardamon, and coriander for 30 seconds. Add the minced ginger root, onions, garlic and sliced chilies and tomatoes. Simmer gently until tomatoes have been reduced to pulp.

4 Return the potato slices to the pan, cover and simmer gently until potatoes are tender. Stir occasionally.

5 When the potatoes are cooked, increase the heat, if necessary, to reduce excess liquid. Shake pan continuously to prevent mixture from sticking.

6 Sprinkle with coriander leaves or parsley.

Serves 4

CREOLE TOMATOES

Make these with the best tomatoes you can find, vine-ripened if possible. The flavour of the fresh tomato counts a lot in this recipe.

Butter	2 Tbsp (25 mL)
Green bell pepper	1 medium, seeded and finely chopped
Fresh red chili pepper	1, seeded and finely chopped
Onion	1 large, finely chopped
Tomatoes	8, peeled and quartered
Tomato juice	1/2 cup (125 mL)
Salt	1/2 tsp (2 mL) or to taste
Freshly ground pepper	1/2 tsp (2 mL) or to taste
Tabasco	a dash, or to taste

1 Melt the butter in a large saucepan. Add the green pepper, red chili, and the onion and cook slowly until the onion is yellow.

2 Add the tomatoes and the tomato juice. Cook slowly for 20 minutes, partially covered. Season to taste with salt, pepper, and Tabasco.

Serves 4

SPICED CHEESE POTATOES

Potatoes are wedged, rolled in cheese and cayenne, and baked crisp in the oven. Serve them as snacks with drinks or as a side dish.

Potatoes	6 medium
Garlic	4 cloves
Salt	1 tsp (5 mL)
Vegetable oil	1/3 cup (75 mL)
Cayenne	2 tsp (10 mL)
Parmesan cheese	1/4 cup (50 mL)

1 Scrub potatoes, then slice lengthwise into 4 wedges. Leave skins on.

2 Crush garlic cloves with salt, then combine with the oil, cayenne, and Parmesan cheese.

3 Toss potato wedges in the oil mixture until evenly coated. Arrange on a rimmed baking sheet. Bake at 375°F (190°C) for 40-50 minutes, or until potatoes are tender and golden brown.

Serves 4

SPINACH WITH CURRIED SPLIT PEA SAUCE

Lentils could easily be substituted in this delicious dish.

Yellow split peas	1/2 cup (125 mL)
Fresh spinach	1 lb (450 g) or 6 cups (1.5 L) packed
Vegetable oil	2 Tbsp (25 mL)
Fennel seeds	1/2 tsp (2 mL)
Ground cumin	1/2 tsp (2 mL)
Ground coriander	1/4 tsp (1 mL)
Crushed dried red chilies	1 Tbsp (15 mL)
Garlic	3 cloves, peeled and minced
Onion	1, chopped
Water	2 cups (500 mL)
Fresh lemon juice	4 Tbsp (60 mL)
Salt	1 tsp (5 mL) or to taste

1 Wash split peas and soak in water for 1 hour.

2 Heat oil in a saucepan and sauté fennel, cumin, coriander, and crushed red chilies until aromatic. Add garlic and onion and fry gently for 5 minutes.

3 Pour in water and bring to a boil. Drain peas and add to pot. Simmer for 1-1 1/2 hours until peas are tender and sauce is fairly thick. Stir in the lemon juice and season with salt.

4 Rinse spinach and chop coarsely. Place in a separate pot, cover and cook over medium heat until spinach is tender, but still bright green (about 3 minutes). Drain well and arrange on a small platter.

5 Pour sauce over spinach and serve immediately.

Serves 4

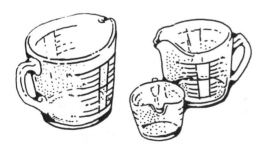

HOT STIR-FRIED VEGETABLES

This dish has a triple spice whammy from the bean paste, chili sauce, and a little from the hoisin sauce. But like many Chinese dishes, it contains sugar, which softens the bite.

Carrots	2, peeled
Sweet red pepper	1
Leeks	1 cup (250 mL) sliced, white part only
Broccoli	3 cups (750 mL) flowerets
Cauliflower	2 cups (500 mL) flowerets
Peanut oil	2 Tbsp (25 mL)
Chicken stock	1/3 cup (75 mL)
Hot bean sauce or paste	1 Tbsp (15 mL)
Hoisin sauce	1 Tbsp (15 mL)
Szechuan chili sauce	1 tsp (5 mL)
Cornstarch	1 1/2 tsp (7 mL)
Dry sherry	1 Tbsp (15 mL)
Sugar	1/2 tsp (2 mL)

1 Cut carrots into thin diagonal slices. Seed pepper and slice into matchstick-sized pieces.

2 Heat wok over medium high heat for 30 seconds. Add the peanut oil and heat until oil is hot, but not smoking. Add carrots and stir-fry for 1 minute. Add the leeks, broccoli, cauliflower and pepper and stir-fry for 2 minutes. Add the chicken stock, hot bean sauce, hoisin sauce, and Szechuan chili sauce.

3 Mix together cornstarch, sherry, and sugar. Pour over vegetables and stir until sauce thickens. Serve immediately.

Serves 4

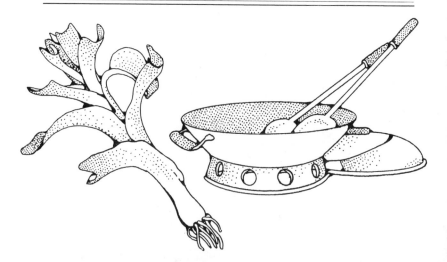

ACHAR

A crunchy hot salad from Singapore served as a first course at the Olé Malacca restaurant in Toronto.

Cucumbers	2, peeled, seeded and cubed
Carrots	2, thinly sliced
Spanish onions	2, cut into 2-inch (5-cm) chunks
Cabbage	1/4 head, 2 cups (500 mL) chopped
Cauliflower	1/4 head, separated into flowerets
Salt	1 1/2 tsp (7 mL)
Dried chilies	8
Shallots	8
Garlic	2 cloves
Fresh ginger root	3/4-inch (2-cm) slice, peeled
Unsalted cashew nuts	3
Dried shrimp	1/2 cup (125 mL)
Vegetable oil	1/2 cup (125 mL)
Mustard seeds	1/2 tsp (2 mL)
Turmeric	1/2 tsp (2 mL)
White vinegar	3/4 cup (175 mL)
Sugar	3 1/2 Tbsp (57 mL)
Salt	1/2 tsp (2 mL) or to taste
Unsalted roasted peanuts	1 cup (250 mL)

1 Place cucumbers, carrots, onions, cabbage, and cauliflower, in a bowl. Sprinkle with salt and let sit for at least 4 hours. Soak dried shrimp in boiling water for 1 hour.

2 When the vegetables are limp, rinse to remove salt. Spread vegetables on a clean, dry towel in a breezy place to dry. Grind together the chilies, shallots, garlic, ginger, and cashews. Drain and pound shrimp with a mortar and pestle.

3 Heat the oil in a large skillet or wok and fry the mustard seeds for 30 seconds before adding ground spices. Fry this mixture for 3-4 minutes and when the ground ingredients separate from the oil, add the pounded shrimp. Continue cooking for another 2-3 minutes before adding vinegar and sugar. Simmer mixture until it is fairly thick, about 10 minutes. Season to taste with salt and more sugar, if desired. Stir in the peanuts.

4 Add the prepared vegetables and toss quickly to mix thoroughly. As soon as the vegetables are well mixed, remove pan from the heat.

5 Chill before serving. This can also be ladled into jars and kept in the refrigerator for several days.

Yields 8-10 cups.

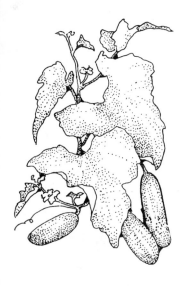

HOT CUCUMBERS

When fresh cucumbers are wilted with hot spice, they surrender some of their raw crunch, but none of their flavor. These are spicy, delicious and meant to be eaten as a condiment — salad with a meal.

Cucumbers	2, unpeeled
Sugar	2 Tbsp (25 mL)
Salt	1/4 tsp (1 mL)
Peanut oil	3 Tbsp (50 mL)
Garlic	2 cloves, bruised
Crushed dried red chilies	2 tsp (10 mL)
Soy sauce	1 Tbsp (15 mL)
Vinegar	2 Tbsp (25 mL)

1 Cut each cucumber in half and remove seeds. Cut each half into 4 strips, then cut each strip into 4 pieces. Combine sugar and salt in a small dish.

2 Heat oil in a wok or skillet over medium heat. Add the garlic and dried chilies and stir-fry until the chilies darken. Increase heat and scatter in the cucumbers. Stir-fry until the skin is bright green. Pour in soy sauce and sprinkle with the sugar and salt mixture. Stir until the sugar has caramelized slightly.

3 Place in a dish. Cool, then cover and chill. Stir several times. When chilled, add the vinegar, toss, and serve.

Serves 4

HOT AND SOUR COLESLAW

Use wine vinegar or plain white vinegar for tartness and chili-pepper oil (recipe in the condiments and relishes section) for the spice-heat. Serve with spareribs.

Cabbage	2 cups (500 mL) finely shredded
Carrot	1/2 cup (125 mL) grated
Onion	1/2, thinly sliced
Green pepper	1/2, seeded and thinly sliced
Salt	1 tsp (5 mL)
Vinegar	6 Tbsp (90 mL)
Chili-pepper oil	3 Tbsp (50 mL)

1 Combine all ingredients and mix thoroughly. Cover and refrigerate for 1 hour.

Serves 4

INDONESIAN PEANUT SALAD

Also called *gado-gado*, this is a wonderful mixture of finely cut vegetables and sliced fruits connected by a peanuty-hot sauce. The sauce itself is quite versatile and may be used as a dressing for cole-slaw or as a dunking sauce for roast meats or raw vegetables.

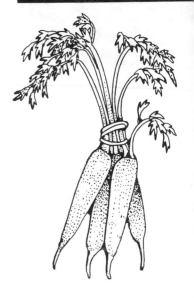

Salad

Alfalfa or bean sprouts	6 cups (1.5 mL), of any desired
Shredded cabbage	assortment
Shredded carrot	
Green bell pepper strips	
Fresh snap peas	
Ripe tomato wedges	
Avocado slices (dipped in lemon juice)	
Mango slices	
Melon chunks	
Pineapple chunks	

Peanut Sauce

Shelled roasted unsalted peanuts	1/2 cup (125 mL), ground in blender
or	
Fresh unsalted peanut butter	1/2 cup (125 mL)
Molasses	2 Tbsp (25 mL)
Soy sauce	2 Tbsp (25 mL)
Garlic	3 cloves, finely minced
Crushed dried red chilies	1 tsp (5 mL)
Fresh lemon juice	2 Tbsp (25mL)
Water	1/2 cup (125 mL)
Peanut oil	1 Tbsp (15 mL)

1 In a small saucepan, combine ground peanuts or peanut butter, molasses, soy sauce, garlic, chilies, lemon juice, and water. Simmer gently for 10 minutes. Remove from heat and stir in peanut oil. Chill.

2 Arrange a selection of fruit and vegetables on a large platter. Serve with the peanut sauce.

Yields about 2/3 cup (150 mL)

PASTA, RICE, BEANS, BREADS

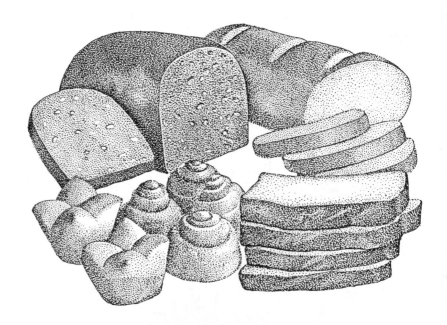

PASTA WITH HOT CLAM SAUCE

Serve this with garlic bread and a full-bodied Italian red wine.

Fresh clams	3 dozen, steamed and chopped
or	
Canned clams	2 cups (500 mL) drained
Olive oil	1/2 cup (125 mL)
Garlic	4 cloves, finely minced
Hot green chilies	4, minced
Mushrooms	1 cup (250 mL) chopped
Fresh tomatoes	1 cup (250 mL) peeled and diced
Dried oregano	1 tsp (5 mL)
Fresh parsley	1/2 cup (125 mL) minced
Salt	1/2 tsp (2 mL) or to taste
Freshly ground pepper	1/2 tsp (2 mL) or to taste
Spaghetti, fettuccini or linguine	1 lb (450 g)
Butter	4 Tbsp (60 mL)
Grated Parmesan cheese	2 Tbsp (25 mL) or to taste

1 Heat oil in a large skillet. Sauté garlic, chilies, and mushrooms for 2 minutes. Add tomatoes and oregano and simmer until sauce begins to thicken, about 5 minutes. Stir in clams and parsley and remove from heat. Season to taste with salt and pepper.

2 In boiling salted water, cook the pasta *al dente*. Drain well and toss with butter.

3 Reheat sauce just to boiling. Serve at once over hot pasta with freshly grated Parmesan cheese.

Serves 4

Beef Cubes with Cayenne and Spinach

SPAGHETTI WITH SWEET AND HOT PEPPERS

Use plum tomatoes, even if they are the canned variety, for this flavourful dish. Their rich taste gives good support to the tastes of the combined peppers, olives, and onions.

Onion	1 medium
Fresh hot green, red, or yellow chili pepper	1 medium
Sweet green pepper	1 medium
Mushrooms	1 1/2 cups (375 mL)
Olive oil	1/4 cup (50 mL)
Wine vinegar	1 Tbsp (15 mL)
Plum tomatoes	2 cups (500 mL) peeled and chopped
Spaghetti	1/2 lb (450 g)
Black olives	1/2 cup (125 mL) pitted and sliced
Salt	1/4 tsp (1 mL)
Freshly ground pepper	1/4 tsp (1 mL)
Italian parsley	2 Tbsp (25 mL) finely chopped

1 Thinly slice onion. Seed peppers and cut lengthwise into strips. Clean and slice mushrooms.

2 Heat olive oil in a saucepan. Sauté the peppers, onion, and mushrooms until limp. Stir in wine vinegar.

3 Add the plum tomatoes and bring to a boil. Lower the heat and simmer, uncovered, for 15 minutes, stirring occasionally.

4 In the meantime, cook the spaghetti in boiling salted water until *al dente*. Drain and place in serving dish.

5 Add olives, salt, and pepper to sauce and stir. Pour sauce over spaghetti, tossing to coat each strand. Sprinkle with parsley and serve immediately.

Serves 4

THAI RICE NOODLES

Called *phat thai*, this typical and exceptionally tasty example of Thai food was provided by the Bangkok Garden Restaurant in Toronto. Many of the ingredients were new to us, though all are available at Oriental specialty stores. The fish sauce, in particular, made us cautious; it smells like old cheese, but when cooked, it has a surprisingly delicate taste.

Dried rice noodles, medium size	4 oz (100 g)
Vegetable oil	1/4 cup (50 mL)
Garlic	2 cloves, finely minced
Raw shrimp	3 Tbsp (50 mL) chopped
Lean ground pork	3 Tbsp (50 mL)
Sugar	1 tsp (5 mL)
Fish sauce (Nam pla)	1 Tbsp (15 mL)
Soy sauce	1 tsp (5 mL)
Hot chili sauce	2 tsp (10 mL)
Eggs	2, beaten
Tamarind sauce	2 Tbsp (25 mL)
Bean sprouts	1/4 cup (50 mL)
Scallion	1, sliced
Salty preserved radish	1 Tbsp (15 mL)
Salted or unsalted peanuts	2 Tbsp (25 mL) coarsely ground
Green onions	2 Tbsp (25 mL) sliced
Lemon	2 wedges
Cucumber	1

1 Soak noodles in hot water for 20 minutes, or until soft. Drain.

2 Heat oil in a wok or large skillet and sauté garlic until golden. Add the shrimp and ground pork and stir-fry until lightly browned. Add the sugar, fish sauce, soy sauce, and chili sauce and stir-fry until the sugar dissolves. Pour in the beaten eggs, let them set slightly, then stir to scramble.

3 Add the noodles and stir-fry about 2 minutes. Push noodles to side of wok or skillet. Add the tamarind sauce and cook for 1 minute. Add the bean sprouts, scallions, radish, and stir-fry until bean sprouts are slightly cooked, about 1 minute. Stir noodles down into tamarind mixture and stir-fry until well-mixed.

4 Pile noodles on a serving dish and sprinkle with peanuts and scallions. Seed cucumber and slice lengthwise into 4 pieces. Place lemon and cucumber wedges on side of plate.

Serves 2

BIRYANI

This is hotter than a classic Indian or Pakistani biryani, which usually is quite mild and a good dish for neophytes to order in an Indian restaurant. Much like a pilau, it is a meal in itself, requiring no accompaniment. Biryani differs basically from a pilau in that the rice is partially cooked before the spiced meat and vegetables are added.

Onions	3, chopped
Butter	1/2 cup (125 mL)
Fresh ginger root	2 Tbsp (25 mL) peeled and minced
Hot green chilies	4
Ground cardamon	1 tsp (5 mL)
Turmeric	1/2 tsp (2 mL)
Ground cumin	1/2 tsp (2 mL)
Ground ginger	1 tsp (5 mL)
Cayenne	1 tsp (5 mL)
Garlic	2 cloves, minced
Ground blanched almonds	1/4 cup (50 mL)
Chicken	1 2-3 lb (1-1 1/2 kg), disjointed
Lean lamb	1 lb (450 g), cut in small cubes
Rice	1 1/2 cup (375 mL)
Powdered saffron	1/2 tsp (2 mL)
Water	3 cups (750 mL)
Cinnamon	1-inch (2.5-cm) stick
Whole cloves	4
Salt	2 tsp (10 mL)
Yoghurt	1/2 cup (125 mL)
Raisins	1/3 cup (75 mL)
Cream	1/2 cup (125 mL)
Lime juice	2 Tbsp (25 mL)
Whole blanched almonds	1/4 cup (50 mL)
Whole cashews	1/4 cup (50 mL)

1 Fry the onions in half the butter until translucent. Add the fresh ginger, chilies, cardamon, turmeric, cumin, ground ginger, cayenne, garlic, ground almonds, chicken and lamb. Fry, stirring often until meat is browned.

2 Meanwhile, boil rice in 3 cups of water with the saffron, cinnamon, cloves and salt for 15 minutes. Drain, but do not remove whole spices. Stir yoghurt into the meat mixture.

3 In a buttered casserole, add 1/3 of the meat mixture, top with 1/3 of the rice and a sprinkle of raisins. Continue layering meat and rice. Melt remaining butter and pour over rice. Cover casserole and bake at 325°F (160°C) for about 45 minutes until rice and meat are tender.

4 Remove casserole from oven and dribble cream and lime juice over top. Garnish top with whole almonds and cashews. Return to the oven, uncovered, for 10 minutes.

Serves 4

RISOTTO WITH SAUSAGES, TOMATO, AND BASIL

A risotto is an Italian dish, made creamy and rich with cheese and slow cooking. The hot sausage and the Italian rice may be purchased at Italian specialty stores.

Unsalted butter	2 Tbsp (25 mL)
Hot Italian sausage	1 lb (450 g), sliced
Onion	1 medium, chopped
Very ripe plum tomatoes	2 cups (500 mL) peeled
Salt	1/2 tsp (2 mL)
Freshly ground pepper	1/2 tsp (2 mL)
Fresh basil	2 Tbsp (25 mL) finely chopped
Short grain Italian rice	1 1/4 cups (300 mL)
Hot chicken broth	2 cups (500 mL)
Chili sauce	2 tsp (10 mL)
Mozzarella cheese	1 1/2 cups (375 mL) grated
Italian parsley	2 Tbsp (25 mL) finely chopped

1 Heat butter in a large saucepan and sauté sausages and onion until sausages are lightly browned. Drain excess fat.

2 In a food processor or blender purée peeled tomatoes and add to sausage mixture. Season with salt, pepper, and basil. Stir in rice, hot broth, and chili sauce. Cover and simmer for 25 minutes, or until rice has absorbed all liquid.

3 Fluff rice with a fork and stir in mozzarella cheese and parsley. Serve immediately.

Serves 4

NASI GORENG

A dish popular throughout Indonesia and Malaysia. Rice is flavoured with molasses, spices, and soy sauce and fried with meat and vegetables. It is served as part of a *ristaffel* — a series of courses in an Indonesian banquet. If served on its own, it is traditionally accompanied by fried egg strips and sliced tomatoes.

Peanut oil	2 Tbsp (25 mL)
Onion	1 medium, chopped
Ground cumin	1/2 tsp (2 mL)
Ground coriander	1/2 tsp (2 mL)
Ground ginger	1/2 tsp (2 mL)
Ground cinnamon	1/4 tsp (1 mL)
Turmeric	1 tsp (5 mL)
Fresh ginger root	1 tsp (5 mL) peeled and finely minced
Crushed dried red chilies	1 tsp (5 mL)
Long-grain rice	1 cup (250 mL)
Hot chicken broth	2 1/4 cups (550 mL)
Vegetable oil	1 Tbsp (15 mL)
Minced pork or shrimp	1 cup (250 mL)
Molasses	1 Tbsp (15 mL)
Soy sauce	2 Tbsp (25 mL)
Roasted peanuts	1/2 cup (125 mL) chopped
Cooked chicken	1 cup (250 mL) cut in thin strips
Scallions	2, chopped
Cooked green peas	1/3 cup (75 mL)
Vegetable oil	4 tsp (20 mL)
Eggs	3 large
Salt	pinch

1 Heat peanut oil in a large saucepan. Sauté onion, cumin, coriander, ginger, cinnamon, turmeric, ginger root, and red chilies for 5 minutes. Add rice and sauté 5 minutes until rice is golden and oil is absorbed. Add the hot chicken broth, cover and simmer for 15-20 minutes until all liquid is absorbed.

2 Heat 1 Tbsp (15 mL) of oil in skillet. When hot, add minced meat and sauté, 5 minutes for pork, 2-3 minutes for shrimp.

3 Stir molasses and soy sauce into the rice. Add the chopped peanuts, chicken, pork or shrimp, scallions, and green peas. Toss gently and let stand, covered, for 5 minutes before serving.

4 To make egg strips, lightly beat the eggs with a pinch of salt. Heat
   a 7 to 8-inch (18 to 20-cm) skillet over moderate heat. Add 1 tsp
   (5 mL) of oil, then pour in one-quarter of the egg mixture. Tilt the
   skillet to cover the bottom with an even layer of egg. Cook for 1-2
   minutes until set. Slide egg sheet onto a plate and let cool. Continue to make the thin egg sheets with remaining oil and egg. Roll
   up each sheet and cut it crosswise into 1/4-inch (5-mm) slices.
   Garnish the top of the nasi goreng with egg strips.

Serves 4

POTATO PANCAKES WITH CHILIES

These are crêpe-like in texture. Try them for lunch or as a first course
with tiny sausages wrapped inside.

Eggs	2
Onion	1 small, quartered
Salt	1 tsp (5 mL)
Flour	2 Tbsp (25 mL)
Baking powder	1/4 tsp (1 mL)
Potatoes	3 cups (750 mL), small cubes
Fresh hot green chilies	4, seeded
Vegetable oil	1/2 cup (125 mL)

1 Put eggs, onion, salt, flour, baking powder, 1/2 cup (125 mL)
   potato cubes, and chilies into blender or food processor. Process
   until mixture is almost smooth. Add remaining potato cubes and
   process until potatoes are cut into tiny chunks.

2 Heat about 2 Tbsp (25 mL) oil in a heavy skillet. Use about 2 Tbsp
   (25 mL) batter for each pancake. Brown well on both sides. Drain
   on paper toweling.

Yields about 12 pancakes

JAMBALAYA

This Cajun dish that hails from Louisiana combines the flavours of smoked meats and hot peppers, with just a whiff of cloves and thyme in a base of long-grained rice. Like all Louisiana Cajun food, it has its origins in New Brunswick. When the French-speaking Acadians settled in Louisiana, their recipes and techniques became known as "Cajun", a derivative of the word "Acadian."

Butter	2 Tbsp (25 mL)
Onions	2, chopped
Green pepper	2, seeded and chopped
Fresh hot chilies	2, seeded and minced
Garlic	4 cloves, minced
Celery	1 stalk, chopped
Boneless pork	1 lb (900 g), cubed
Baked ham	1 cup (250 mL) finely chopped
Smoked sausage	6 small, cut into 1/4-inch (5-mm) slices
Salt	1/2 tsp (2 mL)
Freshly ground pepper	1/2 tsp (2 mL)
Chili powder	1 tsp (5 mL)
Bay leaves	3
Thyme	1/4 tsp (1 mL)
Whole cloves	2
Tomato sauce	1/2 cup (125 mL)
Chicken broth	3 cups (750 mL)
Long-grain rice	1 1/2 cups (375 mL)
Parsley	3 Tbsp (50 mL) finely chopped

1 Melt butter in a large heavy pot over medium heat. Add the onions, green peppers, chilies, garlic, celery, and pork. Sauté over low heat for 15 minutes, stirring frequently. Add the ham and sausage and cook for 5 minutes longer.

2 Sprinkle in salt, pepper, chili powder, bay leaves, thyme, and cloves. Pour in tomato sauce, chicken broth, and rice and bring to a boil. Reduce heat and simmer, covered, for about 20 minutes, or until rice is cooked.

3 Fluff rice with a fork, garnish with chopped parsley, and serve immediately.

Serves 6

BEAN CASSEROLE WITH HOT SAUSAGES AND CHILIES

This hearty meal is rich with flavours of smoked meats, spiced sausage, red wine, and chilies. A crisp green salad and a chilled beer are good accompaniments.

Kidney beans	2 cups (500 mL), soaked overnight in water
Smoked ham	1/2 lb (250 g), cut into bite-size pieces
Italian or hot sausage	1/2 lb (250 g)
Green pepper	1, chopped
Onion	1, chopped
Tomato	1, peeled and finely chopped
Garlic	3 cloves, finely minced
Red wine	1/2 cup (125 mL)
Mild chili powder	2 Tbsp (25 mL)
Crushed dried red chilies	1 tsp (5 mL)

1 Drain the beans and put in a saucepan with enough fresh water to cover them. Bring to a boil, lower heat and simmer until beans are tender, about 1-1 1/2 hours. Drain and save the liquid.

2 Sauté the sausages until brown. In a buttered casserole, place a layer of beans, then a layer of ham and whole sausages, then a sprinkle of green pepper, onion, tomato, and garlic. Repeat these layers.

3 Mix the bean liquid with the red wine, chili powder and crushed red chilies. Pour this over the beans. It may be necessary to add boiling water to completely cover beans. Bake at 350°F (180°C), uncovered, for about one hour. Stir gently once or twice during cooking time.

Serves 4

COUSCOUS WITH CHICK PEAS, VEGETABLES, AND RAISINS

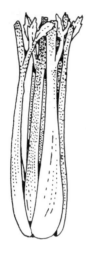

Couscous is the national dish of the north African countries of Morocco, Algeria, and Tunisia. The couscous itself is a fine semolina made from wheat grain that looks much like cream of wheat. Because of its increasing popularity, it can be found in the specialty section of most supermarkets. Basically, the dish consists of semolina steamed over a stew of vegetables or meat. The pot used in its preparation is called a couscousier. The utensil is easily purchased, but it can be simulated by lining a colander with cheesecloth and setting the colander in a larger pot so that it acts like a double boiler. This recipe includes raisins as a sweet contrast to the other savoury ingredients. Couscous may be spicy or not, but it is traditionally served with a very spicy sauce called harissa. Note that the chick peas must be soaked overnight and that the dish takes several hours to prepare.

Chick peas	1/4 cup (50 mL)
Couscous	1 lb (450 g)
Olive oil	2 Tbsp (25 mL)
Boneless lamb	2 lbs (900 g) cubed
Onion	1, quartered
Carrots	2, coarsely chopped
Bay leaves	2, coarsely chopped
Tomato paste	4 Tbsp (60 mL)
Water	6-8 cups (1.5-2 L)
Fresh hot red chilies	2 small, finely minced
Ground cumin	2 tsp (10 mL)
Ground ginger	1 tsp (5 mL)
Cinnamon	1/2 tsp (2 mL)
Salt	1 tsp (5 mL)
Celery	5 stalks, coarsely chopped
Turnip	2 small, peeled and cut in chunks
Sweet potato	1 small, peeled and quartered
Green peppers	2, seeded and quartered
Potato	1 medium, peeled and quartered
Raisins	1/4 cup (50 mL)
Butter	2 Tbsp (25 mL)

1 Soak the chickpeas in water overnight. Drain, cover with fresh water, and cook for 1 1/2 hours. Drain and set aside.

2 Spread the couscous on a deep tray or baking sheet. Sprinkle the couscous with just enough water to dampen the grains. Stir the couscous with your fingers until evenly moistened. Let sit for 15 minutes. Moisten again with more water.

3 In the bottom of a couscousier, heat the olive oil. Sauté the lamb, onion, and carrots until meat just begins to brown.

4 Add chickpeas, bay leaves, tomato paste, and 3 cups (750 mL) water. Cover and simmer for 30 minutes. Now add chilies, cumin, ginger, cinnamon, salt, celery, turnip, sweet potato, green peppers, potato, and raisins. Pour in remaining water, but make sure the liquid level will be below the bottom of the top section of the couscousier.

5 Put the couscous in the top section of the couscousier. Set the top section on the lower one and cover the couscousier with its lid. If necessary, wrap a damp tea towel around the join to seal any leaks. Simmer for 30 minutes. Begin timing from the moment steam escapes from the top of the couscousier.

6 When the vegetables are tender and the couscous is soft and fluffy, remove couscous to a large warm platter. Toss with the butter and ladle some broth over the couscous.

7 Arrange vegetables and meat over the couscous and serve with the rest of the broth and a bowl of harissa sauce (recipe follows).

Serves 6-8·

Harissa Sauce

Dried hot, red chilies	6
Caraway seeds	2 Tbsp (25 mL)
Garlic	2 cloves
Coarse salt	1 Tbsp (15 mL)
Vegetable oil	1/3 cup (75 mL), approximately

1 Soak the chilies in cold water for 1 hour to soften them. Split the chilies and remove the stems and seeds.

2 Pound the chilies in a mortar with the caraway seeds, garlic, and salt until they form a paste.

3 Mix in enough oil to make the paste liquid. To use the sauce, dilute a bit in a spoonful of broth and pour over each serving of the couscous.

Yields approximately 1/2 cup (125 mL)

CORN AND BEAN CHILI

This meatless chili can be served as part of a vegetarian dinner with brown rice, an onion and tomato salad, and guacamole.

Oil	3 Tbsp (50 mL)
Onion	1 large, chopped
Fresh hot green chilies	2, seeded and minced
Mild chili powder	1 Tbsp (15 mL)
Ground cumin	1 tsp (5 mL)
Dried oregano	1/4 tsp (1 mL)
Vegetable broth	2 cups (500 mL)
Tomato paste	2 Tbsp (25 mL)
Fresh or frozen corn kernels	1 cup (250 mL)
Cooked kidney beans	4 cups (1 L)

1 Heat oil in a large saucepan or Dutch oven. When hot, sauté onion, garlic, and green chilies, until onion is soft; do not brown. Add chili powder, cumin, and oregano and cook for 2 minutes.

2 Add vegetable broth, tomato paste, and corn. Mash 2 cups of the kidney beans and add to saucepan, along with whole beans.

3 Cover and simmer for 30 minutes. If chili is not thick enough, simmer, uncovered, for 15 minutes.

Serves 4

GARLIC-CHILI TOAST

Without the chili this extra-garlicky toast packs a wallop; with the chili, it's dynamite. Serve it with bouillabaisse, gazpacho, or spare-ribs.

Butter	1 cup (250 mL)
Garlic	5 large cloves, peeled
Fresh green chilies	1 tsp (5 mL) finely minced
Red chili sauce	1 tsp (5 mL)
French bread	1 loaf

1 In a food processor or blender, whip together butter, garlic, green chili peppers, and red chili sauce.

2 Split loaf lengthwise and spread with butter mixture. Bake at 375°F (190°C) until butter has melted and bread is hot, about 10 minutes.

SPICIER PIZZA

International cooperation is enlisted to give this otherwise traditional pizza pizzaz; a dollop of Szechuan chili sauce (available at Oriental specialty stores) is included in the basic tomato sauce. This is a crispy crust pie with an enticing homemade taste.

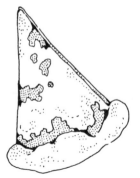

Dry yeast	1 Tbsp (15 mL)
Warm water	1 1/3 cup (325 mL)
Olive oil	4 Tbsp (50 mL)
Salt	2 tsp (10 mL)
Flour	3 1/2-4 cups (875 mL-1 L)
Tomato sauce	2 cups (500 mL)
Dried oregano	2 tsp (10 mL)
Dried thyme	1 tsp (5 mL)
Fennel seeds	1 tsp (5 mL)
Garlic	4 cloves, peeled and pressed
Szechuan chili sauce	2 tsp (10 mL)
Mozzarella cheese	2 cups (500 mL) grated
Parmesan cheese	1 cup (250 mL) grated

1 Dissolve the yeast in 1/3 cup (75 mL) warm water and combine with 1 cup (250 mL) warm water, 2 Tbsp (25 mL) olive oil, salt, and flour. Mix well and knead for 10 minutes. Put in a greased bowl and cover with plastic wrap. Let rise for 2 hours or until double in bulk. Punch down and divide in two. Let rest for 10 minutes.

2 Roll the dough into two 12-inch (30.5-cm) circles. Place on pizza pans and prick all over with a fork.

3 In a bowl, combine 1 cup (250 mL) tomato sauce, oregano, thyme, fennel seeds, garlic, and chili sauce.

4 On each pizza, spread 1 cup (250 mL) tomato sauce, then sprinkle with 1 cup (250 mL) Mozzarella and 1/2 cup (125 mL) Parmesan cheese. Drizzle with 1 Tbsp (15 mL) olive oil. Let sit for 10 minutes. Bake at 400°F (200°C) for 25 minutes until golden brown.

Yields 2-12 inch (30.5-cm) pizzas

CHEESE AND PEPPER BREAD

This savoury bread is good toasted and spread with cream cheese.

Sugar	1 tsp (5 mL)
Lukewarm water	1/2 cup (125 mL)
Active dry yeast	1 Tbsp (15 mL)
Butter	1/4 cup melted, cooled to lukewarm
Eggs	2, lightly beaten
Milk	2 Tbsp (25 mL)
Salt	1 tsp (5 mL)
Freshly ground black pepper	1 tsp (5 mL)
Cayenne	1 1/2 tsp (7 mL)
Old Cheddar cheese	1 cup (250 mL) grated
All-purpose flour	2 1/2 cups (675 mL), approximately

1 Dissolve sugar in water and sprinkle yeast over top. Let stand for 10 minutes. Stir briskly with a fork.

2 In a large bowl mix the butter, eggs, milk, salt, pepper, 1 tsp (5 mL) cayenne and cheese. Beat in the dissolved yeast.

3 Add about 2 1/2 cups (675 mL) flour. Slightly more flour may be needed to make a moderately stiff dough. Turn dough onto a lightly floured board and knead for 5 minutes. Place in a buttered bowl and lightly butter the top of the dough. Cover and let rise in a warm place until double in bulk, about 1 hour. Wash hands thoroughly after handling dough to remove all traces of chili oil.

4 Punch down the risen dough and form into a ball. Cover and let rest for 10 minutes. Form dough into a mound and place on a buttered baking sheet. Butter the top.

5 Cover and let rise until double in bulk, about 45 minutes. Bake at 375°F (190°C) for 25-30 minutes. Brush hot loaf with a little melted butter and sprinkle with remaining cayenne.

Yields 1 loaf

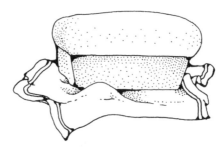

ENCHILADAS

Soft tortillas are filled with onion and cheese, rolled crêpe-style and baked with a hot tomato sauce. Serve with sour cream, chopped onion, and guacamole.

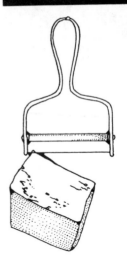

Olive oil	2 Tbsp (25 mL)
Onions	3 medium, minced
Garlic	3 cloves, minced
Fresh hot chilies	2, seeded and minced
Chili powder	2 tsp (10 mL)
Cumin	1 tsp (5 mL)
Tomato sauce	1 cup (250 mL)
Chicken broth	1/2 cup (125 mL)
Vegetable oil	3 Tbsp (50 mL)
Tortillas	12
Monterey Jack cheese	4-5 cups (1-1.25 L) shredded

1 Heat olive oil in a saucepan and sauté 1/2 cup (125 mL) minced onion, garlic, and chili pepper, until onion is soft.

2 Add chili powder and cumin. Sauté for 1 minute. Pour in tomato sauce and chicken broth. Simmer for 5 minutes.

3 Heat vegetable oil in a small frying pan. Dip each tortilla in the sauce, then fry in hot oil for about 10 seconds until it has softened.

4 Fill the centre of each tortilla with 1 Tbsp (15 mL) of minced onion and 1-2 Tbsp (15-25 mL) of shredded cheese. Roll the tortillas and place seam side down in a single layer in an oiled casserole.

5 Pour remaining sauce over top and sprinkle with remaining cheese. Bake at 350°F (180°C) for 15-20 minutes.

Serves 4

CONDIMENTS
AND RELISHES

144

HOT PICKLED LEMONS

This is an unusual and delicious condiment that goes particularly well with stewy dishes like couscous. Once they are prepared, the bottled lemons must sit for at least a week before they are ready to eat.

Lemons	6
Coarse salt	4 Tbsp (60 mL)
Whole dried chilies	6
Bay leaf	1
Vegetable oil	1 1/2 cups (375 mL), approximately

1 Slice lemons 1/4 inch (5 mm) thick and place in a stainless steel or plastic colander (not aluminum). Sprinkle with 2 Tbsp (25 mL) salt. Cover colander with plastic wrap and place over a bowl. Let stand for 24 hours or until lemon slices are limp. If you make this in the summer, place in a sunny window and the process will not take as long.

2 Rinse off salt with cold water. Pack the lemon slices, chilies, and bay leaf in a 1-quart (1-L) jar, sprinkling remaining salt between the layers.

3 Fill jar with vegetable oil. Tap jar on counter to release the air bubbles. Put lid on jar and let stand at room temperature for 1-3 weeks.

Yields 1 quart (1 L)

PAPRIKA RELISH

Hot paprika peppers get a hearty jolt from 35 cloves of fresh garlic.

Dried hot paprika peppers	2 oz (56 g)
Fresh garlic	35 cloves, minced
Vegetable oil	1 1/2 cups (375 mL)
Peeled stewed tomatoes	5 cups (1.25 L), drained and mashed
Salt	1 tsp (5 mL) or to taste

1 In a medium-sized saucepan, cover peppers with water. Heat to boiling and boil for 2 hours. Add more water if necessary.

2 Drain peppers on paper toweling. Cool. Split skins and scrape off pulp and seeds. Discard skins and stems.

3 Sauté garlic in oil. Stir in pepper seeds and pulp. Cook for 3 minutes. Stir in tomatoes, and simmer, uncovered, until mixture is thick, about 30 minutes. Remove excess oil. Season with salt.

4 Serve with bread and cheese.

Yields 3-4 cups (750 mL-1 L)

CHILI AND ALMOND SAUCE

An addictive concoction of chilies, almonds, and garlic that I like on almost everything, but don't miss trying it on chicken, fish or as a substitute for mayonnaise in a sandwich. This recipe is based on a classical Spanish sauce which is so popular that an annual festival is held in its honour.

Olive oil	1/2 cup (125 mL)
Crushed dried red chilies	4 Tbsp (60 mL)
Almonds	1/2 cup (125 mL)
Ripe tomato	1 medium
Sweet red pepper	1, halved and seeded
Red wine vinegar	2 Tbsp (25 mL)
Salt	1 tsp (5 mL)
Onion	1 small, quartered
Garlic	3 cloves, peeled
Toasted bread	1 2-inch (5-cm) slice (optional)

1 In a small saucepan, heat oil, then stir in dried chilies and almonds. Sauté until almonds begin to turn golden and chilies darken. Remove from heat.

2 Broil the tomato and the red pepper halves until lightly charred, to give a smoky flavour. Put in a paper bag to steam for 5 minutes and rub off the skins.

3 In a blender or food processor, combine all ingredients except the toasted bread. Process until smooth. If sauce needs to be thickened, add pieces of toasted bread until desired consistency is reached.

Yields 2 cups (500 mL)

MALAYSIAN CHILI SAUCE

An excellent and authentic sauce contributed by the owners of Olé Malacca, a Malaysian restaurant in Toronto. Use it wherever chili sauce is required, or as a condiment with roast meats and poultry.

Fresh hot red or green chilies	1 lb (450), coarsely chopped
Tomato	1 large, cut in wedges
Garlic	2 whole heads, about 40 cloves, peeled
White vinegar	2/3 cup (150 mL)
Sugar	1/3 cup (75 mL)
Salt	1/4 tsp (1 mL)

1 In a blender or food processor, liquify the chilies, tomato, and garlic. Pour into a saucepan and add vinegar, sugar, and salt. Bring to a boil, then reduce heat and simmer, uncovered, for about 1/2 hour until thick.

Yields 1 pint (500 mL)

GREEN TOMATO-CHILI SAUCE

We like to have this recipe on hand when the green tomato season is here. The sauce is good on steamed rice, tucked into fresh pita with some rare meat, or mixed into scrambled eggs.

Canned green (güero) chilies	1 cup (250 mL)
Fresh serrano chili pepper	1
Green tomatoes	1 lb (900 g)
Garlic	3 cloves, minced
Onion	1 cup (250 mL) minced
Chicken broth	1 1/2 cups (375 mL)
Fresh coriander	2 sprigs, finely chopped
Salt	1/2 tsp (2 mL)

1 Seed chilies and mince. Peel and chop tomatoes.

2 Combine all ingredients in a large saucepan and bring to a boil. Reduce heat and simmer, uncovered, for 10 minutes. Stir frequently.

Yields approximately 4 cups (1 L)

TRINIDAD HOT SAUCE

One bite of this will bring to mind that old saying, "as hot as a fire in a pepper factory." It becomes even hotter as it ages. Try to find the tiny red or green fresh chilies for this one.

Small hot red chilies	1 lb (450 g), 1-inch (2.5-cm) long
Onions	4 large
Salt	4 1/2 tsp (22 mL)
English mustard	3 Tbsp (45 mL)
Paprika	1 Tbsp (15 mL)
Vegetable oil	1/2 cup (125 mL)
White or cider vinegar	2 cups (500 mL)

1 Remove stems from chilies. Mince onions and combine in a non-metallic bowl with chilies, onions, and salt.

2 Add mustard, paprika, and oil and mix well. Heat vinegar to boiling and pour over chili pepper mixture. Mix thoroughly.

3 When cool, mix again and place in sterilized jars. This sauce will keep indefinitely in a cool, dark place. Serve with a wooden or plastic spoon, rather than metal.

Yields approximately 3 pints (1.5 mL)

CHILI-PEPPER OIL

A potent addition to anything that needs hotting up. Store it in a jar in the refrigerator and add a few drops to scrambled eggs, spaghetti sauce, soup, and stews.

Vegetable oil	1 cup (250 mL)
Crushed dried chilies	1/4 cup (50 mL)

1 Heat oil in a small saucepan until hot. Turn heat to low and add crushed chilies. Stir for 1 minute. Remove from heat. When oil is cool, stir then strain through cheese cloth. Store in a small jar.

Yields 1 cup (250 mL)

PEPPER WINE

Use this delicious condiment in whatever savoury dish sherry is required, such as Newburgs or soups. Use the hottest fresh chilies you can find, taking care not to rub your eyes with your hands.

Fresh hot chilies	8 whole, washed and dried
Dry sherry	1 cup (250 mL)

1 Place the whole chilies in a small jar. Pour the sherry over them and seal the jar. Let sit at room temperature for at least 10 days before using.

Yields 1 cup (250 mL)

HOMEMADE CURRY POWDER

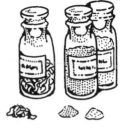

Any Indian cook worth her turmeric will tell you that the yellow-green powder sold in the supermarkets as curry powder has nothing to do with real curry. (''Curry'', in fact, simply means ''sauce''.) Though each of the curry dishes in this book has its own combination of spices included with the recipe, you may wish a combination that can be stored for any dishes you devise yourself.

Turmeric	4 Tbsp (60 mL)
Ground cumin	5 Tbsp (75 mL)
Ground ginger	3 Tbsp (50 mL)
Dry mustard	1 Tbsp (15 mL)
Ground cloves	1 Tbsp (15 mL)
Mace	1 Tbsp (15 mL)
Fennel seeds	1 Tbsp (15 mL)
Peppercorns	2 Tbsp (25mL)
Coriander seeds	5 Tbsp (75 mL)
Crushed dried red chilies	4 Tbsp (60 mL)
Peeled cardamon seeds	1 Tbsp (15 mL)

1 Combine in a bowl, turmeric, cumin, ginger, mustard, cloves, and mace. In a small skillet, lightly toast fennel, peppercorns, coriander, dried chilies, and cardamon. Coarsely grind whole spices in a blender or mortar and pestle. Combine with spices in bowl and mix thoroughly.

2 Store in a small, airtight jar.

Yields 1 1/2 cups (375 mL)

GARAM MASALA

Garam masala is usually used to sprinkle on foods after they are cooked as a seasoning. It may also be used in cooking.

Whole black peppercorns	1/4 cup (50 mL)
Cumin seeds	1/4 cup (50 mL)
Whole dried red chilies	2
Peeled cardamon seeds	1/4 cup (50 mL)
Turmeric	1 Tbsp (15 mL)
Ground mace	2 Tbsp (25 mL)
Ground cloves	2 Tbsp (25 mL)

1 Combine peppercorns, cumin seeds, red chilies, and cardamon seeds in a small ovenproof dish. Roast at 225°F (110°C) for 20 minutes. Grind in a coffee grinder or blender, or pulverize with a mortar and pestle. Blend with the turmeric, mace, and cloves.

2 Store in a small, airtight jar. It will keep its potency, which is considerable, for several months.

Yields 1 cup (250 mL)

JALAPEÑO PEPPER CONSERVE

Find fresh jalapeño peppers, or those not pickled in brine, for this recipe from Betty Singer of San Francisco. This conserve is wonderful with roast lamb or spread on crackers with cream cheese.

Green peppers	4 large
Fresh jalapeño peppers	14-16 medium
Fresh lemon juice	1/2 cup (125 mL)
Cider vinegar	1 cup (250 mL)
Sugar	6 cups (1.5 L)
Liquid pectin	6-oz (170-mL) bottle
Green food colouring	optional

1 Seed and grind the green peppers and jalapeño peppers, or chop them very finely.

2 Combine ground peppers with lemon juice, cider vinegar, and sugar in a heavy 4-quart (4-L) saucepan. Bring to a rolling boil, stirring constantly, and boil for 15 minutes. Add pectin and boil for 5 minutes more.

3 Remove from heat and add green food colouring if desired. Cool slightly, stirring occasionally. Pour into sterilized jars and seal immediately. Let cool and store in a cool dark place.

Yields 3 pints (1.5 L)

JALAPEÑO JELLY

This recipe for jalapeño jelly made with peppers preserved in natural brine is from Karen May of Winnipeg, who notes that the unbriney peppers have a special flavour. I would try both this recipe and the one for Jalapeño Pepper Conserve before you settle on the one that will become a staple in your refrigerator.

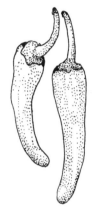

Jalapeño peppers, roasted and peeled, in natural brine	1 4-oz (100-mL) can
Green pepper	1, seeded and chopped
White or cider vinegar	1 cup (250 mL)
Sugar	4 cups (1 L)
Pectin	1 bottle
Green food colouring	a few drops (optional)

1 Drain, seed, and chop the jalapeño peppers. Purée jalapeños and green pepper in a blender or food processor.

2 Combine purée and vinegar in a saucepan and bring to a boil, reduce heat and simmer for 10 minutes.

3 Pour purée into a fine-mesh strainer over a large saucepan. Let drain for 15 minutes. Press gently with the back of a wooden spoon to extract all the liquid. Discard pulp.

4 Add sugar to liquid in saucepan and bring to a boil. Add liquid pectin and boil for 1 minute.

5 Remove from heat and add green food colouring, if desired. Skim off foam and pour into sterilized bottles. Seal immediately.

Yields 4 6-oz (150-mL) jars.

MANGO CHUTNEY

An island of sweet chutney on a plate of hot curry usually provides a welcome oasis. This chutney shows no such mercy. It is as hot as the food it complements. If you can't find under-ripe mangoes, tart green apples will do fine.

Slightly under-ripe mangoes	12
White or cider vinegar	2 1/3 cup (575 mL)
Brown sugar	1 cup (250 mL)
Fresh ginger root	4 inch (10-cm) piece, peeled and finely chopped
Fresh hot chilies	4, finely chopped
Garlic	4 large cloves, peeled and crushed
Raisins (Thompson are best)	3 cups (750 mL)
Onions	2 large, sliced
Salt	1 Tbsp (15 mL)

1 Peel mangoes and slice fruit from the seed. Discard seeds. Chop pulp coarsely.

2 In a large Dutch oven or preserving kettle, heat vinegar and sugar until sugar dissolves.

3 Add remaining ingredients and stir constantly over medium-high heat until chutney is thick, about 30 minutes.

4 Ladle into hot sterilized jars and seal immediately.

Yields approximately 4 pints (2 L)

JANE GALE'S AIOLI

Aioli, a traditional Provençal dressing made of egg yolks, oil, and a lot of fresh garlic, is much like mayonnaise in consistency. It is said to be based on the Valencian *ali oli*. Traditionally, aioli is served with salt cod or in fish soup, but try it with boiled chicken and potatoes too.

Stale white bread crumbs	1 Tbsp (15 mL)
Wine vinegar	1 Tbsp (15 mL)
Garlic	8-10 medium cloves, minced
Salt	1/4 tsp (1 mL)
Egg yolks	4 medium
Vegetable oil, or half olive oil and half vegetable oil	1 1/2 cups (375 mL)
Fresh lemon juice	juice of 1/2 lemon, or 4 1/2 tsp (22 mL)
Cayenne	1/4 tsp (1 mL)

1 Place bread crumbs in a large mortar and pestle or mixing bowl. Moisten with wine vinegar and pound to a paste.

2 Add the garlic and pound until the garlic and bread make a smooth purée. Add salt and egg yolks and stir for a few minutes until very sticky.

3 With a wire whisk begin stirring in oil, drop by drop, until sauce is very thick. Stir in lemon juice and cayenne.

Yields 1 1/2 cups (375 mL)

HORSERADISH DRESSING

This dressing with a bite is good tossed with leftover cold beef or on a salad of shredded lettuce and sliced beets.

Olive oil	3/4 cup (175 mL)
Dijon mustard	1/2 tsp (2 mL)
White or cider vinegar	1/4 cup (50 mL)
Freshly ground pepper	1/4 tsp (1 mL)
Salt	1/4 tsp (1 mL)
Fresh horseradish root	3 Tbsp (50 mL) peeled and grated

1 Place all ingredients in a jar. Replace lid and shake until ingredients are well blended.

Yields 1 cup (250 mL)

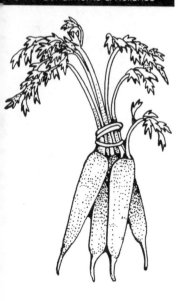

HORSERADISH CREAM

The combination of grated fresh horseradish and moderating cream goes particularly well with smoked fish.

Cream cheese	1/2 cup (125 mL)
Sour cream	1/2 cup (125 mL)
Fresh horseradish root	1/2 cup (125 mL) peeled and coarsely grated
Salt	1/4 tsp (1 mL)

1 Cream cheese should be at room temperature. Beat cream cheese until light, then blend in sour cream.

2 Fold in freshly grated horseradish and salt.

Yields 1 1/2 cups (375 mL)

KIM CHEE

This fiery pickled vegetable is a basic condiment in Korean cuisine, and served as automatically in Korean restaurants as catsup is in North American. So important is the salad, that it has been designated a National Treasure by the South Korean Government. Though kim chee is made from any number of vegetables, including white radish, eggplant, and squash, the most common is pecher, a type of Chinese cabbage. It is very strong and should be approached with caution by the novice.

Chinese cabbage	1 head
Coarse salt	2 Tbsp (25 mL)
Scallions	6, shredded
Garlic	4 cloves, minced
Fresh hot red chilies	3, finely minced
Fresh ginger root	1-inch (2.5-cm) piece, peeled and grated

1 Chop the cabbage coarsely and sprinkle with salt. Let sit for 1 hour, then rinse with cold water to remove salt.

2 Combine cabbage, scallions, garlic, chilies, and ginger root. Place in a large glass jar and add water to cover. Cover tightly.

3 Place in refrigerator for at least 5 days, stirring occasionally.

4 Serve at room temperature for best flavour.

Yields about 6 cups (1.5 L)

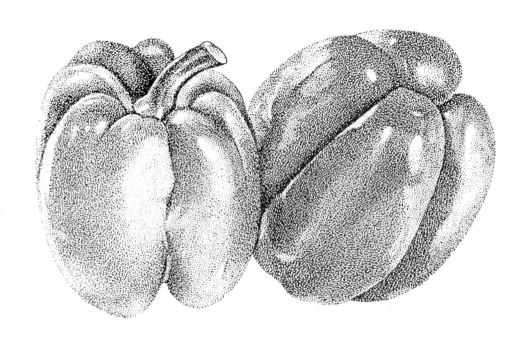

Index

Kitchen Metrics

For cooking and baking convenience, the Metric Commission of Canada suggests the following for adapting to metric measurement. The tables give approximate rather than exact conversions.

SPOONS

1/4 tsp	1 mL
1/2 tsp	2 mL
1 tsp	5 mL
1 Tbsp	15 mL
2 Tbsp	25 mL
3 Tbsp	50 mL

CUPS

1/4 cup	50 mL
1/3 cup	75 mL
1/2 cup	125 mL
2/3 cup	150 mL
3/4 cup	175 mL
1 cup	250 mL

OVEN TEMPERATURE

200°F	100°C	350°F	180°C
225°F	110°C	375°F	190°C
250°F	120°C	400°F	200°C
275°F	140°C	425°F	220°C
300°F	150°C	450°F	230°C
325°F	160°C	475°F	240°C